THE
FOUR SEASONS
SPA CUISINE®

BY

Seppi Renggli

WITH

SUSAN GRODNICK

SIMON AND SCHUSTER
New York

Designed by Levavi & Levavi
Manufactured in the United States of America

10   9   8   7   6   5   4   3   2   1

Library of Congress Cataloging in Publication Data
Renggli, Josef, DATE–
The Four Seasons Spa Cuisine.

Includes index.
1. Low-calorie diet—Recipes.   2. High-protein diet—Recipes.
3. Low-cholesterol diet—Recipes.
I. Grodnick, Susan.   II. Title.   III. Title: 4 Seasons Spa Cuisine.
RM222.2.R46   1986   641.5′635   85-30322
ISBN: 0-671-54440-3

Contents

CONTENTS

Acknowledgments

I would like to thank Susan Grodnick, who worked so closely with me to develop the manuscript for Spa Cuisine. I am especially grateful to my colleague and right hand, Christian (Hitch) Albin, and my dedicated kitchen staff. They have worked hard to make Spa Cuisine at The Four Seasons successful. My heartfelt thanks also to my editor at Simon & Schuster, Carole Lalli.

Foreword

We all know that the American diet is often too high in calories, fat, cholesterol, and salt and too low in certain vitamins and minerals. We have all heard that to reduce the incidence of heart attack, stroke, cancer, diabetes, and osteoporosis (brittle bones) Americans should change their eating habits. But the way we eat is based on long-standing habits and traditions that are very difficult to change. Eating is more than obtaining good nutrition; it is often a time to enjoy good taste and good companionship—and until now the conventional wisdom has dictated that a really first-rate dining experience and good nutrition were incompatible. Spa Cuisine, created by Chef Seppi Renggli and served at The Four Seasons restaurant, has dislodged that attitude. The superb menus (appetizer and main course) that have been delighting New York diners at The Four Seasons for the past three years are now available for you to prepare at home.

Each menu contains only about 700 calories, is relatively high in protein, and low in fat, saturated fat, and cholesterol. In addition, all Spa Cuisine dishes are prepared without added salt and are therefore low in sodium. At the same time, they have been designed to provide adequate amounts of certain nutrients, such as iron, calcium, zinc, and folic acid, which are often in short supply in the American diet. Because they are low in calories, these menus leave room for a simple fresh fruit dessert or a slice of bread (or small roll) or a small salad, all of which will boost the carbohydrate and the fiber content of the meal.

These dishes demonstrate that when the creativity of a master chef is turned loose to stretch our sense of taste while providing us with the best in nutrition, the results are truly remarkable. Spa Cuisine dispels the myth that if it tastes good it can't be good for you. And it achieves this by using fresh foods that are prepared with great imagination and inventiveness.

I hope that the concept of Spa Cuisine will convince you that good living and healthy living *can* go together—and that the menus in this book will give you the added satisfaction of being able to prepare these wonderfully tasty and nutritious dishes yourself.

—MYRON WINICK, M.D.
Director of the Institute for Human Nutrition,
Columbia University's
College of Physicians & Surgeons

Introduction

Seppi Renggli and the two-of-us have been working together for nearly twenty years. And what a glorious adventure it has been! We have explored the diverse cuisines of the world, traveled, opened and closed restaurants. Seppi has been and continues to be our esteemed and beloved associate, without whom The Four Seasons would never have attained its innovative role and its widely acknowledged leadership among the finest restaurants of the world.

Over the years our respect and affection for each other has been the key to our successful collaboration. Together, we examine the new waves (an endless preoccupation) and speculate on the future trends on the culinary horizon. Many new creations and styles and concepts have emerged from our happy reflections and ruminations—but none has been as exciting as Spa Cuisine, an original concept. This dramatic innovation has been brilliantly assembled in this milestone volume, a labor of love and discovery, including over one hundred recipes.

To many, The Four Seasons has always been perceived as a restaurant of unmatched elegance that serves the most singular creations whose sublime taste one could savor for years. People from all over the world have been attracted to our restaurant for its grandeur and ambience, to be sure —but most of all for its inestimable cuisine, so distinctively sensual.

In recent years we have become aware of the fitness revolution, that health and nutrition have become major concerns of our clientele along with the rest of America. For each jogger on Park Avenue, clad in stylish running apparel and Nike footwear, there was a diner at The Four Seasons requesting a mite less salt, a touch less sauce, a shade less meunière, and more and more of our customers were ordering Perrier and lime before dinner.

In early 1983 Seppi Renggli and the two-of-us therefore decided to create a very special selection of dishes that would be nutritionally attractive to this growing legion of customers who shared our belief that superb taste and nutritional integrity could and should go together. Thus we drafted a memorandum, and we reprint here the opening salvo of this prophetic document:

THE CONCEPT: to include in both our Bar Room and Pool Room: low calorie, low sodium, low cholesterol courses which are gastronomically pleasing for: a. composition of flavors; b. texture; c. presentation.

REASONS: a. future trends of health and diet; b. our customers' awareness of nutrition.

We sent this memo to George Lois and Bill Pitts, partners of our advertising agency. We asked them to develop a name for this new cuisine that would not be encumbered by clinical jargon (such as "diet" or "low cal") or by any word or phrase that would suggest a new variable of diet discipline. We were looking for a name for a new family of dishes that would enable nutrition-minded customers to order wonderful meals with a low content of sodium, fats, sugar, and cholesterol. These would certainly not be "diet" dishes, but they would be very nutritional and simply delicious.

In a few days Bill called us to say, "We have the name and it's perfect." He came right over with a small card bearing two words: "Spa Cuisine." We loved the name and promptly registered it for trademark status as the exclusive name of The Four Seasons. (Such status has since been granted.)

We then turned our attention to another "must" in our memorandum:

RECOGNIZED NUTRITION EXPERT: Food preparation to be done with controlled and documented quantities and ingredients with the consultation and approval of a well-known and respected authority on nutrition.

Bill called his son, Peter Pitts, who was working for Cable Health Network, and asked for suggestions of experts on nutrition and health. From his list, we chose Dr. Myron Winick, the Director of the Institute for Human Nutrition at Columbia University's College of Physicians & Surgeons. Bill called Dr. Winick and arranged for us to meet to discuss Spa Cuisine.

Happily, Dr. Winick, a frequent diner at The Four Seasons, was genuinely excited by the possibility of serving as our consultant. He told us of Joyce Leung, a full-time nutritionist on his staff who could work with Seppi Renggli on menu preparation. Dr. Winick set down several criteria in developing Spa Cuisine:

1. Use foods with high nutrient density per calories (e.g., the most vitamins and minerals per calorie intake. Sugar, for example, is high

in calories, but has virtually no nutritive benefits, and therefore provides only "empty" calories).

The focus should be on foods which contain vitamins and minerals not readily available in the diets of a large percentage of the American population: *Vitamins*—folic acid, vitamin B-6, vitamin C; *minerals*—iron, calcium, zinc.

2. Use foods low in fat, saturated fat, and cholesterol (fish, skim milk, etc.).
3. Choose foods low in sodium (but *not* sodium free).
4. Add fiber (vegetables, cereals).
5. Use complementing proteins (corn and beans, rice and beans) to create balanced protein content.

In the fall of 1983, Seppi Renggli began to commute between The Four Seasons and Columbia University, learning about nutrition from Dr. Winick's clinician, Joyce Leung. In January 1984, the first Spa Cuisine creations—three appetizers and two main courses—appeared on the menu. They were designed so the two courses complemented each other to make a nutritionally balanced meal.

Seppi's passionate involvement in Spa Cuisine reflects not only his apprenticeship in Europe as a *régimier*—a cook trained to observe disciplines in cooking and to respect individual clients' diets—but also his deep interest in varied cooking techniques and trends.

As the months went by, Seppi became a chef possessed. He created recipes for seafood, fowl, veal, beef, pork, lamb, and game. All were sent to Joyce Leung for her scientific scrutiny and approval. She analyzed each dish for its protein, carbohydrate, sodium, and fat content, as well as for calories, fiber, cholesterol, calcium, zinc, iron, folic acid, and sucrose. After taking her calibrations, Joyce often returned recipes to Chef Renggli with notations on the need for more calcium and less fat or more zinc and less sodium. Then, after the final okay from nutritionist Leung, Chef Renggli trained our staff of thirty cooks to prepare Spa Cuisine.

At first little or no fanfare ushered in this inspired innovation. Spa Cuisine appeared discreetly on our menu as simply another category of dishes. Since then our Spa Cuisine offerings have been expanded and become more varied. Judging from the enthusiastic response of our many guests and our friends in the media, it was the right idea at the right time in the right place.

We have received hundreds of requests for Seppi's recipes, all masterful blends of superb taste and sensible nutrition. Articles on Spa Cuisine have appeared in newspaper columns and in national magazines; TV stations have sent camera crews into our kitchen; and the restaurant press has fastened onto Spa Cuisine as the culinary phenomenon of the eighties. It was time, we decided, to put all of Seppi's grand creations into a book, this book. It contains most of the Spa Cuisine dishes that have appeared on our menu and many that we plan to serve.

With this book we hope those who have had, and those who have not yet had, Spa Cuisine at The Four Seasons will have the opportunity to see that dining can be at once nutritional and sensual.

TOM MARGITTAI   PAUL KOVI

About the Book

One of the reasons I enjoy cooking so much, especially at The Four Seasons, is that there is always a fresh challenge. There are complete new menus for each season, countless dinners to plan, new ingredients to work with. In making my decisions, I always consider the guests. For some, an all-game dinner is intriguing; other meals feature a seasonal specialty, like baby lamb or goat, letting the rest of the meal take a back seat. For many years, I have responded to the increased interest in health among some of our customers, preparing salt-free, low-cholesterol dishes on request, but when Tom and Paul asked me to make such dinners part of the regular menu, I was delighted by the challenge, but not quite sure how easy it would be to implement.

The first thing I did was sit down with Hitch (Christian Albin), my alter ego in the kitchen, and discuss the various aspects involved. We knew it was possible to create nutritionally balanced meals that tasted good. Most of those, however, fall short of The Four Seasons standards. Our goal was to create meals that would satisfy all the senses and make our guests feel as well treated as ever. At The Four Seasons, we pamper our customers with the quality of our food, service, and presentation. We knew it was important not to lose that with the cholesterol.

Once we had our goals clearly in mind, we concentrated on the technical problems. We discussed cooking methods that require little or no fat, considered spices that would make up for the salt we usually take for granted, made lists of ingredients that were flavorful and healthy and other lists of items to avoid.

It was soon apparent that it was difficult, if not impossible, to create a single dish nutritionally balanced in all categories. Working with Joyce Leung, a nutritionist, we developed menus, now set at three each season, that combined an appetizer and main course to give a meal lower in calories than usual with reduced sodium and cholesterol, increased iron, zinc, and other nutrients. One dish may have all the protein, the other all the carbohydrates. Sometimes the calories will be divided evenly between them. More often, the division is unequal.

So, the nutritional balance is found in the menu, not within individual dishes. For that reason, the recipes here are arranged in menus that come as close as possible to achieving that ideal balance.

The decision to omit desserts was mine. Aside from fresh fruit and fruit salads, most low-calorie, healthy desserts are made with substitutes for sugar, cream, and eggs, products I am not happy working with. I much prefer eating an apple than apple pie that is artificially sweetened. If your meal is not complete without dessert, consider a platter like the Sliced Summer Fruits with Mango Puree (page 240). Remember, of course, that it will add calories, cholesterol, and fat.

Developing dishes with little cooking fat was easy for me. Steaming is a superb way to cook, leaving foods flavorful and moist. Years ago, I discovered that plastic wrap makes an ideal seal for many foods, keeping the juices in while not affecting the flavor. Cabbage and lettuce leaves work in the same way.

Of course, boiling in water is virtually fat free and even meat stocks add little fat. Soups make excellent Spa Cuisine dishes. You can grill and broil without fat but it is a little trickier since foods cooked that way can dry out. Spray or rub some oil on the grill before heating to keep the food from sticking.

Another way to cut down on fat is to use nonstick or well-seasoned pans. The best seasoned pans are cast iron, heavy, and inexpensive. They have an added benefit because traces of the iron come off into whatever you cook, adding nutrition. Once seasoned, these pans do need to be treated carefully. Wash them without scrubbing and be sure to dry thoroughly (preferably over heat) to keep them from rusting.

You can also use less oil than called for in most recipes if you use one of the spray oils on the market or spread the oil on with a pastry brush. It lets you coat the pan with much smaller amounts than is possible when you spoon or pour it in. Be sure the oil is hot before adding the food to be seared. Cold fat is absorbed much more quickly than hot, making the final dish oilier because you have to add more to keep food from sticking.

When I first started cooking dishes for Spa, my biggest challenge was finding satisfactory substitutes for salt. I turned to peppers, long my favorite seasoning, as well as ginger and garlic. For those used to bland salt-free diets, some of these dishes may be too spicy. In that case, cut down on the sharper flavors, use less marinade and less pepper.

I also found that by browning onions and shallots a bit, not cooking them just until translucent as so many recipes suggest, they give off more flavor. Garlic, however, becomes bitter when brown, so I do not cook it as long.

The nutritional information given for each menu was calculated for the specific ingredients listed according to weight. We have broken down that nutritional information so that you can judge each recipe accurately and follow any diet, be it low-calorie or low-salt.

The key to the nutritional abbreviations is: CAL, calories; PRO, protein; CHO, carbohydrates; FAT, total fat in recipe; SAT, total saturated fat in recipe; CHOL, cholesterol; FIBER, fiber; CA, calcium; ZN, zinc; FE, iron; FOLATE, folic acid; NA, sodium; SUC, sucrose. The nutrients are measured in grams (g), milligrams (mg), or micrograms (mcg).

If you want to be exact about the nutrients in your diet, I suggest you use a kitchen scale to measure the exact amounts of the ingredients called for in the recipes. Then you can be sure that the nutritional information will match up as well. Weight is a more accurate measure than cups and spoons, which is why it is given for most of the ingredients in the recipes.

Although these recipes are exact, I consider them a guide to a way of thinking about food. In many cases, you can substitute other ingredients and keep the spirit of Spa Cuisine. A beautiful head of broccoli is better than woody asparagus; fresh chicken is preferable to old pheasant. Such substitutions will vary the nutritional values given, but probably not significantly.

A Word About Ingredients

Since I love eclectic cooking, my favorite ingredients include some not usually found in American homes or markets. Most of those called for in these recipes are either Indonesian (sambal ulek, ketjap manis, lemongrass) or Japanese (soba, kombu, bonita flakes). They can be found in oriental shops or health-food stores. All have long shelf lives, except fresh lemongrass, but the dried (sereh) is a fine substitute.

Recipes for the frequently used stocks are in the chapter at the end. The others are included in the specific menu.

Wine

Most customers at The Four Seasons enjoy a glass or two of wine with their meals. We have not calculated the value of such imbibing in our menus, but most have room for the 87 calories in a 3½ ounce glass of dry wine, red or white. It has few nutrients worth the bother of calculating.

Salt

We do not add salt to any Spa Cuisine dishes in the kitchen, although occasionally we add a little low-sodium soy sauce. Since many foods have sodium in them, the final dishes are not sodium-free but are low in sodium, usually well below the RDA. Unless you are on a restricted diet, you can add salt at the table and still have less than the RDA of 667 milligrams for the meal (2,000 milligrams per day). A teaspoon of salt has 5 grams sodium.

Peppers

One of the New World's greatest contributions to the culinary world is the pepper, first brought to Europe by Christopher Columbus. It is fitting, therefore, that these all-American vegetables be among my favorite ingredients in creating dishes for The Four Seasons, a true American restaurant. I cube them to garnish soups, puree them for sauces, roast them for salads. When I find a new pepper, my mind starts racing with thoughts of new dishes in which to use it.

All the vegetable peppers (as opposed to peppercorns which are in the spice category) are related, being of the family *Capsicum*. For years, the bell peppers we knew were red or green. Now I use crates of bright yellow ones, the sweetest of all. There are also the hot peppers, even more essential to my Spa Cuisine cooking than for dishes on the regular menu. I find that the flavor of jalapeño and other pungent peppers partially compensates for the lack of salt.

In most cases, I use only the flesh, discarding the seeds, veins, and core. The veins and seeds of hot peppers are the hottest part, which may cause mouths to burn and even blister. When handling any hot pepper, be careful to wash your knife, cutting board, and hands so the oils don't get onto other foods. The oils may stay on your skin even after washing, so don't rub your eyes or they may sting. If you are very sensitive, wear gloves when handling peppers.

The heat of peppers varies enormously. It is measured in Scoville heat units, ranging from zero units for bell peppers to 2,500 to 4,000 for jalapeño and 60,000 to 80,000 for Tabasco. More mature plants have more pungency, and those grown in warm climates tend to be hotter than those grown in the cold. You cannot, unfortunately, judge the heat by appearance. Neither can you assume that one mild pepper means the whole batch, or even the plant, is mild. My only caution is to taste a bit before you use it. If the pepper is very hot, you'll know by just touching the cut skin to your lip.

I use jalapeño peppers most of the time because they are readily available to me. These smooth, dark green peppers are oval shaped, about two inches long. They grow in the South and Southwest of the United States. Should they not be available in your market, there are many substitutes. Most popular are serrano chilies, commonly used throughout Mexico and the Southwest. They vary considerably depending on where they are cultivated. There are three varieties, all hot. Those most readily available in markets are called Tipico. They look very much like jalapeños except the sides are slightly straighter.

Among the hottest peppers are cayenne, small skinny peppers that come to a point at the end. Often called chili or finger peppers, they are green when young, red when mature. They are fairly easy to grow at home for those who love to garden (as I do) or without easy access to fresh peppers.

You might also find Fresnos, grown in the Southwest where they are often simply called hot chilies. Bright red when mature, they are often used green for cooking. Almost triangular in shape, the Fresno has smooth skin.

If you can't find fresh peppers in your local market, or want to try other varieties, plant them in the sunniest part of your garden.

Although I usually prefer fresh peppers, I sometimes like dry for variety. The dry red chili peppers I use in these recipes are fips, often sold as an ornamental pepper. They are very hot, especially with the veins and seeds. You might prefer to use only half a pepper or to remove the veins and seeds. Dry, round Cascabels are also good. If neither is available, use red pepper flakes, a teaspoon or two for a pepper. As with any dry herb or spice, buy only small quantities at a time so they stay fresh. Avoid any that are musty, stale, or faded.

A Note About Techniques

Most often when recipes call for peeled peppers, the peppers are roasted first so that the charred skin will come off easily. To peel raw peppers, use a vegetable peeler. With a small knife, divide them lengthwise into their natural sections. Remove and discard the core, seeds, and ribs. With a paring knife, cut away any bits of peel that are too difficult to get at with the peeler.

The easiest way to peel tomatoes is to first bring a pot of water to a boil. Remove the core and cut an x on the bottom of each tomato. Drop the tomatoes in boiling water and cook just until the skin starts to come away from the pulp. Do not let the tomatoes get too soft. Remove from the heat and rinse under cold water. Pull off the skin. For most recipes, cut tomatoes in half crosswise and squeeze out the seeds.

An attractive way to cut vegetables is to "turn" them, trimming pieces about 2 inches long and ½ inch wide into ovals. With a paring knife, cut small curving pieces off the ends and along the length to make it roughly the shape of a football. It may take some practice to get the pieces uniform.

THE
SPA CUISINE
MENUS

◇Chicken Gumbo
◇A Timbale of Bay Scallops in Spinach

The chicken gumbo complements the scallop and spinach timbale in its pool of silky red sauce. You can make the gumbo and pepper sauce a day ahead. Assemble the timbales earlier in the day you mean to serve them and let them steam while you eat the gumbo.

Chicken Gumbo   CAL 275

Pro. 21.4 g, Cho 18.2 g, Fat 13 g, Sat 0.1 g, Chol 59.3 mg, Fiber 1.4 g, Ca 64.4 mg, Zn 1.8 mg, Fe 2 mg, Folate 38.1 mcg, Na 71.1 mg, Suc 1.3 g

A Timbale of Bay Scallops in Spinach CAL 168

Pro 21.3 g, Cho 18.6 g, Fat 3.2 g, Sat 0.2 g, Chol 36.2 mg, Fiber 2.8 g, Ca 182.2 mg, Zn 1.9 mg, Fe 5.7 mg, Folate 199.2 mcg, Na 259.8 mg, Suc 0.3 g

Total Menu   CAL 443

Pro 42.7 g, Cho 36.8 g, Fat 16.2 g, Sat 0.3 g, Chol 95.5 mg, Fiber 4.2 g, Ca 246.6 mg. Zn 3.7 mg, Fe 7.7 mg, Folate 237.3 mcg, Na 330.9 mg, Suc 1.6 g

◇Chicken Gumbo

This excellent gumbo will horrify natives of New Orleans who know that a true gumbo must be made with a thick roux of flour and fat. Few others will complain. Okra is a natural thickener, giving both Creole flavor and texture. The final dish has a nice green color.

1 2-pound chicken
1 tablespoon corn oil
1 dry red chili pepper
1 jalapeño pepper, cored, seeded, and sliced
1 cup (¼ pound) chopped onion
⅓ cup (1 ounce) sliced celery
1 cup (3½ ounces) 1-inch-wide strips green bell pepper
3 cloves garlic, minced
¼ cup wild pecan rice
¼ teaspoon ground coriander
¼ teaspoon ground cumin
5 ounces okra, stems removed, cut into ¼-inch rounds (about 1¼ cups)
1 teaspoon gumbo filé powder

Pull any lumps of fat out of the chicken and discard. Put the chicken into a pot, cover with cold water, and bring to a boil. Lower the heat and simmer, partially covered, until the chicken is cooked, 35 to 40 minutes. Remove the chicken from the pot and set aside to cool. Reserve the stock.

When the chicken is cool enough to handle, pull off and discard the skin. Pull the meat from the bones, removing any trace of fat. Cut the meat into 1-inch pieces. Remove any fat from the chicken stock; if you have less than 1 quart, add water. If you have more, bring the stock to a boil and cook until reduced to a quart.

Heat the oil in a 3-quart pot. Add the red and jalapeño peppers, onion, celery, bell pepper, and garlic. Cook for 3 minutes, just to soften. Add the rice, coriander, and cumin. Stir to mix well, then add the reserved stock.

Cook for 15 minutes. Add the okra and cook 15 minutes longer. Add the chicken and simmer for 2 minutes, or until everything is hot. Stir the filé into the soup.

Serves 4

◇A Timbale of Bay Scallops in Spinach

This is a beautiful dish with bright green spinach contrasting with gossamer scallops and red pepper puree.

1 pound bay scallops
1 tablespoon minced jalapeño pepper
1 teaspoon minced orange rind
2 ounces (½ cup) minced shallots
1 clove garlic, minced
1 medium red or yellow bell pepper
¾ pound trimmed leaf spinach, blanched, drained, and squeezed dry
½ recipe Red Pepper Puree Sauce (see below)

Carefully pull the tough muscle off the side of each scallop and discard. Place the scallops in a bowl with the jalapeño pepper, orange rind, shallots, and garlic. Let them marinate a few hours or overnight in the refrigerator.

Cut the bell pepper into its natural sections, discarding the core and seeds. Remove the skin with a vegetable peeler. With a small knife, cut out 4 even rounds of pepper about 1 inch in diameter. Place one, peeled side down, in the center of the bottom of a 1-cup flat-bottomed, heat-proof dish. Arrange 5 scallops in an even circle around the pepper. Prepare 3 more dishes in the same way. Divide half the spinach among the dishes, pressing down so it holds the scallops and pepper in place. Make sure the spinach also covers the sides of the dishes. Fill each dish with the remaining scallops and top with the remaining spinach.

About 15 minutes before you are ready to serve, heat some water in the bottom of a steamer. Place the prepared dishes on the steamer rack, cover, and cook for 10 minutes.

While the timbales cook, heat the pepper puree sauce.

When the timbales are done, remove them from the steamer. Loosen each one by running a knife around the inside edge. Tip each dish to pour out any liquid that may have accumulated on the sides. Spoon some sauce onto each of 4 plates to make a neat circle. Unmold a timbale in the center of each.

Serves 4

◇Red (or Yellow) Pepper Puree Sauce

When made with red peppers this silky sauce will be vibrant, excellent with many fish and chicken dishes. The rich yellow version contrasts well with green and red vegetables. This is an easy sauce to make. If you like, prepare it as long as three days ahead. It can be easily doubled or tripled to give you leftovers for another dish.

4 medium red or yellow bell peppers, cored and seeded
1 small (3-ounce) onion
1 clove garlic, crushed
1 small piece fresh or dried hot pepper
1 tablespoon walnut oil
1 tablespoon red wine vinegar
1 tablespoon fresh lemon juice

Roughly chop the bell pepper and onion. Place them in a heavy pot with the rest of the ingredients. Bring to a boil, cover, and lower the heat so the mixture simmers. Cook for 30 minutes. The mixture should be very soft. Uncover and let it cool to room temperature.

Put the cooled mixture into a food processor or blender and puree until smooth. Then press the sauce through a fine sieve to eliminate bits of skin.

Makes 1½ cups

◇Pepper Pot Soup
◇Wellfleet or Sea Scallops
with Spring Vegetables

You can make the hearty pepper pot soup ahead. Add the bell peppers, tomato, and final seasoning when you reheat it. Since scallops continue to give off liquid as they sit, eventually getting dry and rubbery, cook them at the last minute. The rich soup will sate your guests' hunger while they wait.

Pepper Pot Soup   CAL 180

Pro 19.8 g, Cho 16.2 g, Fat 4.7 g, Sat 1.2 g, Chol 57.8 mg, Fiber 3 g, Ca 174.9 mg, Zn 1.8 mg, Fe 3.5 mg, Folate 60.8 mcg, Na 91.1 mg, Suc 1 g

Wellfleet or Sea Scallops with Spring Vegetables   CAL 230

Pro 29.3 g, Cho 18.5 g, Fat 2.4 g, Sat 0 g, Chol 54.2 mg, Fiber 2 g, Ca 276.6 mg, Zn 2.1 mg, Fe 6.7 mg, Folate 108.7 mcg, Na 358.5 mg, Suc 0.6 g

Total Menu   CAL 410

Pro 49.1 g, Cho 34.7 g, Fat 7.1 g, Sat 1.2 g, Chol 112 mg, Fiber 5 g, Ca 451.5 mg, Zn 3.9 mg, Fe 10.2 mg, Folate 169.5 mcg, Na 449.6 mg, Suc 1.6 g

◇Pepper Pot Soup

This soup is said to have its origins with General Washington at Valley Forge. Tripe seems to have fallen out of favor among Americans since then, which is a shame. In my home, it is considered a delicacy. It is one dish, however, that I feel needs a little salt to bring out the flavor. Unless your diet doesn't allow for any sodium at all, add a bit of salt just before serving.

3/4 pound tripe, trimmed of all fat

2 teaspoons corn oil

1 medium (5-ounce) onion, diced

2 cloves garlic, minced

2 teaspoons red pepper flakes

1/2 teaspoon dried thyme

1 small (1 1/2-ounce) parsnip, peeled and cut into 1/2-inch cubes

3 cups water or stock

1 medium (6-ounce) tomato, peeled, seeded, and cut into 1-inch chunks

1 medium red bell pepper, cored, seeded, and cut into 1-inch squares

1 medium yellow bell pepper, cored, seeded, and cut into 1-inch squares

1 medium green bell pepper, cored, seeded, and cut into 1-inch squares

1/8 teaspoon freshly grated nutmeg

1/2 cup chopped fresh parsley

Put the tripe in a pot with cold water to cover. Bring to a boil and cook for 2 minutes. Drain and pat dry. With a small knife, scrape off any remaining bits of fat. Cut the tripe into 1-inch squares. Set aside.

Heat the oil in a 3-quart pot. Add the onion, garlic, red pepper flakes, thyme, and parsnip. Cook until lightly browned, about 5 minutes. Add the tripe and water or stock. Bring to a boil, partially cover, and lower the heat so the liquid is at a steady simmer. Cook until the tripe is soft, about 2½ hours. Add the tomato and bell peppers. Cook 15 minutes longer.

Stir in the nutmeg and parsley. Serve hot.

Serves 4

◇Wellfleet or Sea Scallops with Spring Vegetables

Wellfleet scallops are sold with the red roe still attached to each scallop. Although not generally available, they turn up in better fish stores from time to time. I prefer them because the roe is so attractive. It also often bursts, turning the sauce a pretty pink. When I use regular sea scallops, I toss in some cherry tomatoes to add color.

¼ pound carrots, cut into rounds
¼ pound turnips, cut into batonettes
¼ pound zucchini, sliced diagonally into ovals
¼ pound broccoli flowerettes
1½ pounds Wellfleet or sea scallops
¼ cup dry vermouth
Juice of 1 lime
Rind of 1 lime, cut into thin strips
3 large (2 ounces) shallots, sliced
1 jalapeño pepper, cored, seeded, and cut into thin strips
¼ cup fresh tarragon leaves
2 cups Fish Stock, reduced to ¾ cup
2 cups watercress leaves, blanched, drained, and squeezed dry
¼ pound cherry tomatoes
Freshly ground black pepper

Bring a large pot of water to a boil. Add the carrots and cook until just done, about 3 minutes. Drain and set aside. In the same water, cook the turnips, zucchini, and broccoli in separate batches. Cook each vegetable until it is done but still crisp. Either keep them warm until ready to serve or cook them ahead and reheat in a steamer or by dipping briefly in boiling water.

Remove and discard the small muscle attached to each scallop.

Bring the vermouth and lime juice to a boil in a 10-inch skillet along with the lime rind, shallots, jalapeño pepper, and tarragon. Cook for 2 minutes, or until the liquid has almost evaporated. Add the scallops and cook over high heat for about 3 minutes. Cover and cook a minute longer. The scallops should be barely done.

With a slotted spoon, remove the scallops to a colander over a bowl, returning any liquid that collects to the skillet. Add the reduced fish stock and cook until further reduced to about ½ cup. Return the scallops to the pan along with the watercress and cherry tomatoes. Add freshly ground black pepper to taste. Cook just to heat through.

Place the scallops and watercress in the center of a platter. Arrange the blanched vegetables neatly around the edge.

Serves 4

NOTE: You can use vegetables other than those indicated. Try to use at least three and vary their shapes and colors. Possible choices include broccoli stems, yellow squash rounds, turban squash, sugar snap peas, snow peas (halved on the diagonal), and cauliflower flowerettes.

◇Baked Pepper and Artichoke Salad
◇Fillet of Red Snapper Braised in Endive and Leek

Peppers and artichokes, standard ingredients in Italian antipasti, make a satisfying first course to serve at room temperature or while the artichokes are still warm. You can cook the fish and rice ahead and keep them warm until just before serving. Then assemble the plates while someone else clears the first course.

Baked Pepper and Artichoke Salad   CAL 158

Pro 9.8 g, Cho 36.3 g, Fat 4.4 g, Sat 0.5 g, Chol 0 mg, Fiber 7.8 g, Ca 133.2 mg, Zn 1.4 mg, Fe 3.9 mg, Folate 148.9 mcg, Na 188.8 mg, Suc 0 g

---

Fillet of Red Snapper Braised in Endive and Leek   CAL 366

Pro 35.1 g, Cho 32.8 g, Fat 8.9 g, Sat 0.9 g, Chol 76.9 mg, Fiber 2.7 g, Ca 244.6 mg, Zn 1.7 mg, Fe 6.2 mg, Folate 353.4 mcg, Na 159.7 mg, Suc 0 g

---

Total Menu   CAL 524

Pro 44.9 g, Cho 69.1 g, Fat 13.3 g, Sat 1.4 g, Chol 76.9 mg, Fiber 10.5 g, Ca 377.8 mg, Zn 3.1 mg, Fe 10.1 mg, Folate 502.3 mcg, Na 348.5 mg, Suc 0 g

---

◇Baked Pepper and Artichoke Salad

Artichokes are a delicious vegetable, most often served whole with dipping sauces, a messy dish. I like them this way, serving only the edible part. I even cut up the bottom and reassemble it on the plate to make it easier to eat.

4 5-ounce artichokes
1 lemon, halved
1 cup (5½ ounces) fresh peas
½ recipe Roasted Peppers as prepared for Roasted Peppers,
*   Buckwheat Noodles, and Chicken Salad (see page 116)*

Cut the stem off one artichoke. Cut away the top leaves in a single chop so you have a piece about 1 inch thick. This is the bottom. Pull off any remaining leaves or parts of leaves. With a paring knife, cut away all the remaining parts of leaves until you reach the pale green bottom. With the same knife or a spoon, pull out and discard the hairy choke. Rub the trimmed bottom with the cut lemon to keep it from discoloring. Repeat with the other artichokes.

Bring a pot of water to a boil. Squeeze the cut lemon into the water and throw in the rinds. Add the artichoke bottoms and cook until tender, about 8 minutes. Drain and rinse briefly under cold water. Put the peas in the same water and cook until just done, about 3 minutes. Drain and rinse.

Pat the artichoke bottoms dry. If necessary, trim each bottom so it can lie flat, open side up. Keeping the shape of the bottoms, cut each into thin strips. Place one bottom in the center of each of 4 individual plates, open sides up, so they look uncut. Arrange alternating strips of roasted red and yellow peppers around each artichoke. Sprinkle peas over the artichokes, letting some spill onto the peppers.

Serves 4

◇Fillet of Red Snapper Braised in Endive and Leek

In this delicate dish, the snapper is wrapped in the leek and endive. The dark watercress leaves provide a sharp flavor and a dark contrast to the pale ingredients.

1 long leek, blanched in boiling water for 2 minutes, drained, and patted dry

8 ¼-pound endives, cooked in boiling water for 20 minutes, drained, and patted dry

½ cup (1 ounce) packed watercress, blanched in boiling water for 2 minutes, drained, squeezed dry, and chopped

4 5-ounce pieces red snapper fillet

1 tablespoon minced jalapeño pepper

1 teaspoon minced orange rind

4 teaspoons minced fresh horseradish

1 recipe Pecan Rice (see below)

Preheat the oven to 350° F.

You need four 1-cup heatproof bowls or ramekins.

Cut the root from the leek and discard. Separate the leaves. Then line each bowl with 3 12-inch-long strips so that they cross in the center of the bottom and drape over the edge, dividing the bowl into 6 equal parts.

Cut the roots off the endives and separate about half of them into individual leaves. Line each bowl with overlapping leaves so the points meet in the center. Set about 24 whole endive leaves aside. Cut the remaining endives into 1-inch pieces.

Place a quarter of the watercress into each lined bowl. Place a snapper fillet on top of each mound of watercress. Fill in the space around the fish with the endive pieces. Sprinkle an equal amount of jalapeño pepper, orange rind, and horseradish on each fillet. Cover with a layer of whole reserved endive leaves. Fold the overhanging leaves and the ends of the leek strips over the top to make neat packages. Cover each bowl tightly with good-quality plastic wrap.

Place the bowls in a baking dish filled with enough water to come halfway up the sides of the bowls. Bring the water to a boil on top of the stove, then place the pan in the oven and cook for 15 minutes. Remove the pan from the oven, but let the dishes stand for 20 additional minutes in the water bath. Remove the plastic wrap. Place an individual serving plate over a bowl and invert the bowl and plate together. Remove the bowl. Repeat with the other bowls. Serve immediately with the pecan rice.

Serves 4

◇Pecan Rice

Wild pecan rice is something of a misnomer. Not wild and not studded with pecans, it is a flavorful rice developed in Texas that does smell of pecans. It is distributed around the country, usually in supermarkets or gourmet food shops. If you cannot find it, substitute regular long- or short-grain (not instant) rice.

2 tablespoons olive oil
¼ cup (1 ounce) minced shallots
½ jalapeño pepper, cored, seeded, and minced
½ clove garlic, minced
½ cup wild pecan rice
1¼ cups Chicken Stock
1 small bay leaf
1 clove

Heat the olive oil in a 1-quart saucepan. Add the shallots, pepper, and garlic. Sauté until lightly browned. Add the rice and cook until well mixed. Add the chicken stock, bay leaf, and clove. Bring the liquid to a boil. Cover the pan, lower the heat, and simmer for 30 minutes, or until done. Discard the bay leaf and clove.

Serves 4

◇Whole-Wheat Linguine with Breast of Quail
◇Braised Fillet of Red Snapper with Spring Onions

Pastas are among my favorite dishes. In this case, the tiny quail breasts go well with the substantial whole-wheat pasta. If you have all the ingredients ready, the pasta can be done in a few minutes. The fish takes a bit more time, but little of it at the stove.

Whole-Wheat Linguine with Breast of Quail   CAL 334

Pro 14.7 g, Cho 43 g, Fat 11.5 g, Sat 2.6 g, Chol 28.9 mg, Fiber 1.9 g, Ca 108.8 mg, Zn 2.1 mg, Fe 4 mg, Folate 35.5 mcg, Na 41.9 g, Suc 0 g

Braised Fillet of Red Snapper with Spring Onions   CAL 347

Pro 35.4 g, Cho 24.1 g, Fat 8.8 g, Sat 0.9 g, Chol 77.2 mg, Fiber 3.2 g, Ca 47.6 mg, Zn 2.4 mg, Fe 4.3 mg, Folate 83.3 mcg, Na 278.2 mg, Suc 0.6 g

Total Menu   CAL 681

Pro 50.1 g, Cho 67.1 g, Fat 20.3 g, Sat 3.5 g, Chol 106.1 mg, Fiber 5.1 g, Ca 156.4 mg, Zn 4.5 mg, Fe 8.3 mg, Folate 118.8 mcg, Na 320.1 mg, Suc 0.6 g

◇Whole-Wheat Linguine with Breast of Quail

Pasta has an affinity for just about any other ingredient. For this recipe, I chose quail breasts set off by bright green sugar snap peas, a newly developed cross between snow peas and sweet peas. You will probably have to bone the breasts yourself, though your butcher might be willing. Let your fingers do most of the work, after using a small knife held against the breast bone to get started. The legs and carcasses are very small. Freeze them to add to your next pot of chicken stock. If you can't get quail, use the breasts from Cornish hens, cut into strips.

Vegetable Stock
½ pound sugar snap peas, sliced diagonally into ½-inch strips
½ pound fresh whole-wheat linguine
¼ pound (4 whole) boneless quail breasts
2 tablespoons olive oil
4 cloves garlic
¼ cup (1 ounce) chopped shallots
Freshly ground black pepper
¼ cup chopped cilantro (fresh coriander)
¼ cup low-fat sour cream
½ 2.5-ounce package 2-Mamina (Japanese radish sprouts)

Bring the vegetable stock to a boil. Put the sugar snap peas in a strainer and cook them in the stock until done, about 2 minutes. Drain and rinse under cold water.

Drop the linguine into the boiling stock. Cook until barely done, about 3 minutes. Drain and rinse under cold water. Set aside.

The piece of meat that often comes away from the breast is the fillet. Pull it from each half breast and cut the larger pieces in two.

Heat the oil and garlic in an 8-inch skillet. Cook for a minute, then remove and discard the garlic. Add the shallots and cook until brown, about 1 minute. Add the quail and freshly ground black pepper. Sauté for 1 minute. Add the sugar snap peas and chopped cilantro. Cook another minute. The quail should be medium rare. Add the linguine and toss to coat, then stir in the sour cream. Do not let it completely mix; some white should streak through.

Arrange the pasta on plates and garnish with 2-Mamina.

Serves 4

◇Braised Fillet of Red Snapper with Spring Onions

Red snapper is a particularly flavorful fish. Cooking it in liquid keeps it moist, making the base for this excellent sauce at the same time.

2 tablespoons corn oil

¼ teaspoon red pepper flakes

¼ cup sliced shallots

1 cup scallions cut into ¼-inch diagonal slices

4 5-ounce skinless red snapper fillets

½ teaspoon fennel seeds, or ¾ cup thinly sliced fennel

2 cups (¼-pound) roughly chopped mushrooms (chanterelle, shiitake, oyster, button), or use ½ ounce dried tree ear, shiitake, etc.

¼ cup Sauternes

1 cup Fish Stock

1 pound snow peas

2 teaspoons arrowroot

Freshly ground black pepper

1 tablespoon low-salt soy sauce

Pour 1 tablespoon oil in a 10-inch skillet. Spread it to coat the bottom, Sprinkle in the pepper flakes, shallots, and ¼ cup scallions. Arrange the fish, skinned side up, in the pan in a single layer. Sprinkle the fennel seeds or fennel on top with the rest of the scallions, the mushrooms, wine, and stock.

Cover the pan and bring the liquid to a boil over medium-high heat. Lower the heat and let simmer for 10 to 12 minutes. Remove the pan from the heat and set aside for a few minutes.

While the fish is cooking, drop the snow peas in boiling water for 2 minutes. Drain and rinse under cold water and set aside.

Remove the fish onto a warm platter, turning each piece over carefully and leaving the vegetables that adhere to it. Spoon the other vegetables around the fish on the platter. Cover and keep warm.

Return the pan to the heat and bring the liquid to a boil. Cook until reduced to ½ cup. If the fish gives off any liquid as it sits, add it to the pan. Put the arrowroot in a small bowl with 1 teaspoon water and stir until the arrowroot is dissolved. Whisk it vigorously into the pan. When the sauce is thick and smooth, spoon it over the fish.

Heat the remaining tablespoon oil in another skillet. Add the snow peas and cook to heat through. Add fresh pepper to taste and the soy sauce. Toss to blend. Serve the snow peas with the fish.

Serves 4

◇Vegetable Ragout Braised in Savoy Cabbage with Velouté of Green Peas
◇Escalope of Striped Bass with Eggplant

Over the years, I have stuffed cabbage with all kinds of meats and seafood but this vegetable stuffing is one of my favorites. You can prepare it early in the day along with the velouté and pepper puree, leaving only the fish and eggplant to concentrate on once your guests arrive.

For a leisurely meal, plan to cook the fish after the first course has been cleared. If you are short of time, start the fish cooking just before sitting down. Keep it warm until you've eaten the cabbage rolls. Return to the kitchen to cook the eggplant, reheat the snow peas, and assemble the dish.

Vegetable Ragout Braised in Savoy Cabbage with Velouté of Green Peas   CAL 340

Pro 19.9 g, Cho 41.8 g, Fat 6.1 g, Sat 1 g, Chol 8.7 mg, Fiber 3.2 g, Ca 157.5 mg, Zn 2.9 mg, Fe 5.9 mg, Folate 132.9 mcg, Na 370.4 mg, Suc 2 g

Escalope of Striped Bass with Eggplant   CAL 337

Pro 30.1 g, Cho 33.6 g, Fat 7.3 g, Sat 1.5 g, Chol 62.2 mg, Fiber 5.2 g, Ca 85.5 mg, Zn 2.2 mg, Fe 5.1 mg, Folate 101.7 mcg, Na 167.3 mg, Suc 1.7 g

Total Menu   CAL 677

Pro 50 g, Cho 75.4 g, Fat 13.4 g, Sat 2.5 g, Chol 70.9 mg, Fiber 8.4 g, Ca 243 mg, Zn 5.1 mg, Fe 11 mg, Folate 234.6 mcg, Na 537.7 mg, Suc 3.7 g

◇Vegetable Ragout Braised in Savoy Cabbage with Velouté of Green Peas

Ham seems an appropriate flavor for the stuffing served with the green pea sauce since I always add ham to split pea soup.

4 large savoy cabbage leaves (½ pound)
1 tablespoon corn oil
1 cup (¼ pound) chopped onion
1 cup (2 ounces) leek greens, cut into ¾-inch squares
2 cloves garlic, minced
1 jalapeño pepper, cored, seeded, and minced
1 cup (¼ pound) diced carrots
1 cup (5 ounces) diced broccoli stems
1 cup (3 ounces) diced celery
1 cup (¼ pound) ¼-inch-thick okra slices
2 ounces smoked ham, cut into ½-inch cubes
1 cup Chicken Stock
Velouté of Green Peas (see below)
4 teaspoons low-fat sour cream
¼ cup diced or sliced red bell pepper

Bring a large pot of water to a boil. Add the cabbage leaves and cook until soft, about 15 minutes. Drain well and set aside.

Preheat the oven to 375° F.

Heat the oil in a 10-inch nonstick skillet. Add the onion, leek, garlic, and jalapeño pepper. Cook for a few minutes until lightly browned. Add the carrots, broccoli, celery, okra, and ham along with ½ cup stock. Cover and simmer for 15 to 20 minutes. Uncover and cook 10 to 15 minutes more. The vegetables should be soft and all the liquid absorbed.

Pare along the center vein of each cabbage leaf so it is fairly flat. Place the leaves, outside down, on your work surface. Divide the vegetable mixture among them. Fold the bottom of each leaf over the mixture, then fold over one side. Roll up each leaf and push the open side in with your finger. Place each roll, seam side down, in a 10-inch pie plate or baking dish. Add the remaining ½ cup chicken stock. Cover the pan with foil and bake for 30 minutes.

Heat the velouté and spoon some of it onto each of 4 heated salad plates. Place a cabbage roll in the center. Spoon a little of the cooking liquid on top to moisten. Add a dollop of sour cream and a few pieces of red pepper. Place the remaining red pepper pieces in the sauce.

Serves 4

◇Velouté of Green Peas

This luscious green sauce, so good with cabbage rolls, adds interest to a platter of steamed vegetables. You can also thin leftover sauce with stock or water for soup.

¾ cup green split peas, soaked overnight in water to cover
1½ jalapeño peppers, cored, seeded, and minced
¾ cup chopped red onion
2 cloves garlic, minced
6 tablespoons chopped celery
6 tablespoons chopped green pepper
3 cups Chicken Stock

Drain the peas and put them into a pot with the remaining ingredients. Bring to a boil, then cover, and lower the heat to a simmer. Cook until everything is soft, about 1¼ hours. Uncover and let cool, then puree in a food processor. Press the mixture through a sieve for a silky puree.

Makes 2½ cups

◇Escalope of Striped Bass with Eggplant

I use the small, skinny oriental eggplants for this dish. The shape echoes that of the fillets, and there are very few bitter seeds. The red sauce gives an otherwise pale dish a splash of color.

1 pound sugar snap peas
Freshly ground black pepper
1 pound skinless striped bass fillets, cut diagonally into 8 2-ounce
*   pieces, each about 1 inch thick*
1 cup Fish Stock, reduced to ¼ cup
¼ cup dry vermouth or dry white wine
1 jalapeño pepper, cored, seeded, and cut into 4 thin slices
1 teaspoon thinly sliced fresh ginger
½ cup thinly sliced shallots
¼ cup water
1 pound eggplant (preferably long oriental), cut lengthwise into 8
*   ¼-inch strips*
1 recipe Red Pepper Puree Sauce (see page 28)

Bring a pot of water to a boil. Add the snap peas and cook for about 2 minutes, or until just done. Drain and keep warm.

Grind black pepper on the fish pieces. Arrange them in a single layer in a 10-inch skillet. Add the reduced fish stock and vermouth along with the jalapeño pepper, ginger, and shallots. Cover the pan and place over high heat. Cook for about 4 minutes. The fish should be just done. If not, cook a minute longer. Uncover the pan and cook 30 seconds longer. Remove the fish and its sauce to a warm plate, being careful not to break the fillets.

Add the water and eggplant slices to the same pan. Cover and cook over high heat for 1 minute. Turn the eggplant slices over and cook until done, about another minute.

To serve, spoon the red pepper puree on individual plates. Alternate 2 pieces of fish with 2 slices of eggplant so they overlap on one side of the plate. Spoon some of the fish sauce on top. Arrange the snap peas on the other side.

Serves 4

◇Stuffed Artichoke Bottom with Mushrooms and Bulgur Wheat
◇Cold Striped Bass with Mango and Papaya

When the weather gets warm, it's nice to have dishes that require minimal time standing over hot burners and near hot ovens. All the cooking for this menu is quick and almost all can (even should) be done ahead, allowing you to be relaxed before your guests arrive. In the end you only need to bake the artichokes and assemble the fish platter.

Stuffed Artichoke Bottom with Mushrooms and Bulgur Wheat   CAL 151

Pro 8.8 g, Cho 35 g, Fat 4.1 g, Sat 0.4 g, Chol 0 mg, Fiber 6.2 g, Ca 130.7 mg, Zn 0.9 mg, Fe 3.5 mg, Folate 105.2 mcg, Na 54.1 mg, Suc 0.4 g

Cold Striped Bass with Mango and Papaya   CAL 368

Pro 34.1 g, Cho 42.8 g, Fat 5.7 g, Sat 1.7 g, Chol 85.2 mg, Fiber 3.2 g, Ca 128.1 mg, Zn 2.4 mg, Fe 4.4 mg, Folate 92.3 mcg, Na 163.6 mg, Suc 17.7 g

Total Menu   CAL 519

Pro 42.9 g, Cho 77.8 g, Fat 9.8 g, Sat 2.1 g, Chol 85.2 mg, Fiber 9.4 g, Ca 258.8 mg, Zn 3.3 mg, Fe 7.9 mg, Folate 197.5 mcg, Na 217.7 mg, Suc 18.1 g

◇Stuffed Artichoke Bottom with Mushrooms and Bulgur Wheat

This is excellent by itself as a first course. You can also serve it with grilled chicken for a main course. Sometimes I make extra bulgur and mushroom stuffing and serve it by itself as a side dish.

1 ounce (2 rounded tablespoons) bulgur wheat

4 8-ounce artichokes

½ lemon

½ clove garlic

½ jalapeño pepper, cored and seeded

¼ teaspoon dry thyme

4 fresh mint leaves, or ¼ teaspoon dry mint

1 tablespoon corn oil

½ cup (2 ounces) diced onion

1 cup (2 ounces) diced leek

2 ounces mushrooms, chopped

2 ounces fresh shiitake, chopped, or ¼ ounce dried, soaked until soft, squeezed dry, and chopped

½ ounce dried porcini, very finely chopped or ground in a spice grinder

¼ cup Chicken Stock

Place the bulgur in a bowl. Add boiling water to generously cover. Let the bulgur soak for 30 minutes until it is fluffy and tender. Drain off the excess water.

Cut the stems off the artichokes. Cut away the top leaves so each piece is about 1 inch thick. These are the bottoms. Pull off any remaining leaves. With a paring knife, trim all the remaining parts of the leaves until you reach the pale green bottoms. With the same knife or a spoon, pull out and discard the hairy chokes. If necessary, trim each bottom so it can lie flat, open side up. Rub the trimmed bottoms with the cut lemon.

Bring a pot of water to a boil. Squeeze the cut lemon into the water and throw in the rind. Add the artichoke bottoms and cook until tender, about 8 minutes. Drain and rinse briefly under cold water. Pat the artichoke bottoms dry.

Chop together the garlic, jalapeño pepper, thyme, and mint until very fine.

Heat the oil in an 8-inch skillet. Add the onion, leek, and chopped seasonings. Sauté for about 2 minutes, or until everything is light brown. Add the chopped mushrooms and shiitake. Sauté 2 minutes longer. Add the porcini and bulgur and cook for another minute. Remove from the heat and let cool.

Preheat the oven to 375° F.

Divide the bulgur mixture in 4 and firmly press one rounded portion into each artichoke bottom. They will be very full. Place them, bottoms down, in a baking dish. Pour the chicken stock in the bottom of the dish. Bake for 5 minutes, or until brown on top and heated through.

Serves 4

◇Cold Striped Bass with Mango and Papaya

This is a beautiful summer dish, the cool, golden fish graced by the lush golden fruit, sweet and juicy.

¼ cup red and green bell pepper slices
¼ cup sliced leek green
¼ cup sliced fennel bulb
1½ teaspoons thin jalapeño pepper slices
1 generous tablespoon sliced shallot
¼ teaspoon saffron threads (optional)
4 5½-ounce pieces striped bass fillet
¼ cup dry vermouth or white wine
1 cup Fish Stock
1 large (1¼-pound) papaya
1 large (1¼-pound) mango
4 radicchio leaves
4 cupped Boston lettuce leaves
12 arugula leaves
1 2.5-ounce package 2-Mamina (Japanese radish sprouts)
100-gram (3.5-ounce) package enoki mushrooms

Preheat the oven to 425° F.

Mix together the bell pepper slices, leek, fennel, jalapeño pepper, and shallot. Place in a 9-inch Pyrex pie plate.

Rub the saffron threads over the top (boned) side of each fish fillet. Place the fillets in a single layer, saffron side down, over the vegetables. Pour in the vermouth and fish stock. Place the pie plate over a flame tamer and slowly bring to a boil, about 3 minutes. Put the plate in the oven and cook for 6 minutes. Remove from the oven and let cool at room temperature, then refrigerate. The liquid will gel.

When you are ready to serve, peel the papaya and mango. Cut the papaya in half and scoop out and discard the seeds. Cut each half lengthwise into 4 even pieces. Cut 2 large slices off the mango, one on either side of the large pit. (Save the pulp around the pit for puree.) Cut each large piece of mango into 4 long slices.

Down one side of an oval serving platter arrange the papaya so that the pieces overlap. Put the mango, also overlapping, down the other side of the platter. Place a radicchio leaf in the center of each cupped Boston lettuce leaf. Arrange 3 arugula leaves attractively on top. Place the 4 lettuce cups at the top of the platter. Arrange the 4 fish fillets, boned side up, overlapping down the center of the platter, between the rows of fruit. Spoon the gelled liquid over the fish. Place a bunch of 2-Mamina under each fillet on one side. Place a bunch of enoki mushrooms under each fillet on the other side. The effect should be of an abstract butterfly.

To serve, give each person one fillet, 2 pieces of mango, 2 of papaya, one lettuce cup, and a bunch of enoki and 2-Mamina.

Serves 4

◇Whole-Wheat Fettuccine with Garlic and Basil
◇Sautéed Dover Sole with Pearl Onions, June Peas, and Romaine

This is a menu for the early days of summer when tiny sweet peas first appear in your (or your neighbor's) garden along with aromatic basil leaves. If you prepare the vegetables and fettuccine ahead, there will be little to do when your guests arrive except assemble the pasta and cook the fish.

Whole-Wheat Fettuccine with Garlic and Basil   CAL 313

Pro 13.7 g, Cho 40.3 g, Fat 11.7 g, Sat 3 g, Chol 11.4 mg, Fiber 2.2 g, Ca 192.8 mg, Zn 1.7 mg, Fe 6.1 mg, Folate 23.9 mcg, Na 157.9 mg, Suc 0 g

Sautéed Dover Sole with Pearl Onions, June Peas, and Romaine   CAL 352

Pro 33.2 g, Cho 22.8 g, Fat 11.7 g, Sat 2.1 g, Chol 83.9 mg, Fiber 1.9 g, Ca 133 mg, Zn 1.5 mg, Fe 3.4 mg, Folate 138.2 mcg, Na 244.9 mg, Suc 4 g

Total Menu   CAL 665

Pro 46.9 g, Cho 63.1 g, Fat 23.4 g, Sat 5.1 g, Chol 95.3 mg, Fiber 4.1 g, Ca 325.8 mg, Zn 3.2 mg, Fe 9.5 mg, Folate 162.1 mcg, Na 402.8 mg, Suc 4 g

◇Whole-Wheat Fettuccine with Garlic and Basil

I like the notion of Italian fettuccine with Italian Parmesan and cubes of Japanese tofu. Being able to meld ethnic ingredients in this way is one of the pleasures of working at The Four Seasons.

Vegetable Stock
½ pound string beans, cut into 1½-inch pieces
½ pound fresh whole-wheat fettuccine
1 tablespoon olive oil
1 tablespoon minced jalapeño pepper
1 teaspoon minced garlic
1 cup chopped fresh basil leaves
2 tablespoons (½ ounce) pine nuts (pignoli)
¼ pound tofu, cut into ½-inch cubes
¼ cup low-fat sour cream
¼ cup chopped fresh chives or scallion greens
1 ounce grated Parmesan cheese

Bring the vegetable stock to a boil. Put the string beans in a strainer and hold in the stock until barely done, about 3 minutes. Drain under cold water, pat dry, and set aside.

Bring the stock back to a boil and add the fettuccine. Cook until barely done, about 3 minutes. Drain and rinse under cold water, reserving ¼ cup stock.

Heat the olive oil, jalapeño pepper, garlic, basil, string beans, and pine nuts in an 8-inch skillet over medium-high heat. Add the reserved stock along with the fettuccine and tofu. Toss to mix well, then add the sour cream. Mix quickly, but not completely. Some white streaks should show. Serve immediately on heated plates. Sprinkle the chives and Parmesan cheese on top.

Serves 4

◇Sautéed Dover Sole with Pearl Onions, June Peas, and Romaine

S̲imply flavored with orange rind and juice, the sole is extraordinarily delicious. At The Four Seasons, we are able to get whole Dover sole. Should you ever be fortunate enough to have a whole fish, use it here. If not, Boston sole, gray sole, Rex sole, sand dab, flounder, or any other flatfish will do admirably.

1 cup Fish Stock, reduced to ½ cup
¼ pound peeled pearl onions or frozen pearl onions, defrosted
¾ pound fresh June peas or frozen peas, defrosted
¼ pound romaine lettuce, cut into ¼-inch strips
1 teaspoon arrowroot
4 Dover soles, fins and tails cut off, interior bones left intact, each
    weighing 10 ounces, or 2 10-ounce Boston sole or other flat fillets
1 navel orange
Freshly ground white pepper
1 tablespoon almond oil

Bring the reduced stock to a boil. Add the onions and cook for 5 minutes. Add the peas and lettuce and cook 1 minute longer. Mix the arrowroot with a little liquid to dissolve, then stir it into the vegetables. Cook for about 30 seconds to thicken. Set the vegetables and sauce aside and keep warm.

If you are using the whole fish, cut down until you reach the bones in the middle. Then cut along the center membrane the full length of the fish. Turn the fish and cut it the same way on the other side. This will make it easier to bone after the fish is cooked. In the same way, if you are using fillets, separate each into 2 pieces by cutting along the center membrane. Using a fine hand grater, grate orange rind onto one side of each fish or fillet. Grind white pepper on top. Turn the fish and add more rind and pepper to the other side.

Heat the almond oil in a 10-inch nonstick skillet (or use 2 smaller skillets) over high heat. (The fish should fit in a single layer.) Halve the orange and squeeze the juice of one half over the fish. Put the fish in the hot pan and cook until browned on the bottom. With a long spatula, carefully turn each piece and cook on the other side until done. Fillets should take about 4 minutes altogether, the whole fish with bones, 10 to 12 minutes.

Serve one large piece of fillet per person, first side up, with some of the vegetables. If serving the whole fish, place it on your work surface with the second (not so pretty) side up. Carefully bone it by cutting down the loosened center with a long, thin spatula and then moving across the fish against the bones to free one piece. Place it, browned side down, on the plate. Remove the other top piece in the same way and place it next to the first to reshape the fish without its bones. Lift out and discard the main bone, now exposed. Scrape against the exposed fillets to be sure to remove all the little bones. Carefully lift up the 2 remaining fillets and place them, browned side up, over the 2 on the serving plate. Spoon some of the vegetables next to the fish on the plate.

Squeeze the juice of the rest of the orange over the fish just before serving.

Serves 4

SAUTÉED DOVER SOLE WITH PEARL ONIONS, JUNE PEAS, AND ROMAINE

◇Buckwheat Noodles in the Oriental Manner
◇Baked Swordfish Steak with Olives and Scallions

The most time-consuming part of the noodle dish is assembling all the ingredients. Although the nutritional values will differ somewhat, the noodles will be equally good with dozens of variations so it is not essential to use exactly the ingredients called for here. Should you prefer, cook everything except the soba ahead, cover, and keep warm. Just before serving, boil the soba, drain it, and toss with the sauce to reheat.

You can also assemble the swordfish on the baking dish and blanch the chard earlier in the day. It will keep your final time in the kitchen to a minimum.

Buckwheat Noodles in the Oriental Manner   CAL 351

Pro 18.7 g, Cho 35.6 g, Fat 14.8 g, Sat 2.5 g, Chol 42.7 mg, Fiber 1.2 g, Ca 88.8 mg, Zn 2.5 mg, Fe 3.7 mg, Folate 62.1 mcg, Na 231.7 mg, Suc 0.5 g

Baked Swordfish Steak with Olives and Scallions   CAL 252

Pro 25.9 g, Cho 13.1 g, Fat 10.8 g, Sat 2.2 g, Chol 61.2 mg, Fiber 1.9 g, Ca 189.4 mg, Zn 1.7 mg, Fe 5.5 mg, Folate 79.5 mcg, Na 323 mg, Suc 0 g

Total Menu   CAL 603

Pro 44.6 g, Cho 48.7 g, Fat 25.6 g, Sat 4.7 g, Chol 103.9 mg, Fiber 3.1 g, Ca 278.2 mg, Zn 4.2 mg, Fe 9.2 mg, Folate 141.6 mcg, Na 554.7 mg, Suc 0.5 g

◇Buckwheat Noodles in the Oriental Manner

Every country has at least one dish made from leftovers. In America, by way of Britain, there are hashes. In Indonesia, there is nasi goreng, fried rice, and ba'mie goreng, mixed noodles. Since the leftovers vary, there is no absolute recipe for either dish. This is my version of ba'mie goreng, as taught to me by my wife. Of course, in the restaurant we make this "leftover" dish from scratch. Feel free to make substitutions if you have true leftovers.

½ pound soba (Japanese buckwheat noodles)

3 tablespoons corn oil

3 ounces cabbage, shredded

2 ounces onion, sliced

1 jalapeño pepper, cored, seeded, and cut into thin slices

1 ounce carrot, cut into julienne strips

1 clove garlic, minced

1 teaspoon sambal ulek (Indonesian chili paste) or dry red chili
    peppers

2 ounces lean pork tenderloin, cut into ¼-inch-wide strips

2 ounces skinless, boneless chicken breast, cut into ¼-inch-wide
    strips

2 ounces shelled, deveined shrimp, halved

2 ounces lean ham, cut into ¼-inch-wide strips

¼ pound bok choy, cut diagonally into ⅛-inch-thick strips

1 large (2-ounce) stalk celery, cut diagonally into ⅛-inch-thick
    strips

1 cup soybean sprouts

1 tablespoon ketjap manis (Indonesian soy sauce)

¼ teaspoon ground cumin

¼ teaspoon ground coriander

¼ teaspoon curry powder

1 teaspoon minced fresh lemongrass

Bring a large pot of water to a boil. Add the soba and cook until done, about 4 minutes. Drain and set aside. This can be done ahead or while the vegetables are cooking.

Heat the oil in a large wok. Add the cabbage, onion, jalapeño pepper, carrot, and garlic along with the sambal ulek. Let sit for about 2 minutes, stirring only occasionally, so everything browns. Add the pork and cook a minute, then add the chicken, shrimp, and ham, one at a time, stirring them in. (If you add everything at once, the pan will cool off too much and the mixture will get watery.)

When everything has lost its raw look, add the bok choy, celery, and bean sprouts. Cook a minute and add the ketjap, cumin, coriander, curry, and lemongrass. Add the drained noodles and cook until they absorb most of the liquid.

Serves 4

⋄Baked Swordfish Steak with Olives and Scallions

I love the strong taste of olives with fish and sometimes smother swordfish in an olive puree. This milder version is very popular at The Four Seasons.

1 teaspoon olive oil

4 5-ounce swordfish steaks, about ¾ inch thick

8 green olives, pitted and coarsely chopped (¼ cup)

8 black Greek olives, pitted and coarsely chopped (¼ cup)

⅓ cup chopped fresh parsley

¼ cup chopped fresh dill

½ cup chopped scallions

1 teaspoon minced jalapeño pepper

Juice of 1 lemon

1 cup salt-free tomato juice

1 recipe Braised Swiss Chard (see below)

Preheat the oven to 450° F.

Lightly oil a heatproof serving platter (a metal sizzling platter that fits into a wooden board is ideal). Place the swordfish steaks on it in a single layer. Top each with an equal part of the olives, parsley, dill, scallions, and jalapeño pepper. (You can mix everything except the pepper together first. Be sure the pepper is evenly distributed among the steaks.)

Squeeze lemon juice on top of each piece of fish, then gently pour over the tomato juice, taking care to keep the herbs and olives from falling off. The juice should be about ½ inch deep in the platter.

Place the platter on top of the stove and bring the liquid to a boil. Place in the oven and cook for 6 minutes. Serve the fish with the tomato liquid as the sauce, accompanied by the braised Swiss chard.

Serves 4

◇Braised Swiss Chard

In this recipe, the soft dark green part of the chard becomes almost a
sauce for the firm white ribs.

1 pound Swiss chard
1½ teaspoons corn oil
1 clove garlic, minced
¼ cup minced shallots
½ jalapeño pepper, cored, seeded, and sliced
½ cup Veal Stock

Bring a large pot of water to a boil. Wash the chard well. Cut the green parts from the white ribs. Drop the green into the boiling water and cook for 4 minutes. Drop the chard into cold water to stop the cooking. Drain, pat dry, and coarsely chop.

Cut the white ribs into 3-inch pieces. Drop them into the same boiling water. Cook for 15 minutes. Cool in cold water. Drain and pat dry.

Heat the oil in a 2-quart pot. Add the garlic, shallots, and jalapeño pepper. Cook for 2 minutes, or until lightly browned. Add the greens and sauté for a minute. Add the stock and cook 5 minutes more. Add the white stems and cook 4 to 5 minutes longer.

Serves 4

◇Whole-Wheat Linguine with Crisp Spring Vegetables
◇Grilled Fillet of Trout with Oysters and Herb Sauce

The delicately flavored vegetables pair well with the grilled trout served with oysters cooked in their own herb sauce. These dishes are best done as they are served, but if the vegetables are prepared ahead, your time in the kitchen will be relatively short.

Whole-Wheat Linguine with Crisp Spring Vegetables   CAL 212

Pro 6.2 g, Cho 33.3 g, Fat 6.7 g, Sat 2.2 g, Chol 8.6 mg, Fiber 1.8 g, Ca 86.9 mg, Zn 1.5 mg, Fe 2.1 mg, Folate 60 mcg, Na 53.8 mg, Suc 0 g

Grilled Fillet of Trout with Oysters and Herb Sauce   CAL 380

Pro 40.3 g, Cho 17.4 g, Fat 15.9 g, Sat 2.2 g, Chol 73.4 mg, Fiber 2.4 g, Ca 564.3 mg, Zn 2.9 mg, Fe 7.4 mg, Folate 64 mcg, Na 217 mg, Suc 0.7 g

Total Menu   CAL 592

Pro 46.5 g, Cho 50.7 g, Fat 22.6 g, Sat 4.4 g, Chol 82 mg, Fiber 4.2 g, Ca 651.2 mg, Zn 4.4 mg, Fe 9.5 mg, Folate 124 mcg, Na 270.8 mg, Suc 0.7 g

◇Whole-Wheat Linguine with Crisp Spring Vegetables

There are pastas for every season. When the first beautiful vegetables start appearing in the market in spring, I use them for dishes like this one, a variation of Italian pasta primavera. Choose what is best that day.

¼ pound fresh whole-wheat linguine
1 tablespoon olive oil
2 large (2 ounces) shallots, thinly sliced
1 clove garlic, minced
1 jalapeño pepper, cored, seeded, and minced
3 ounces carrot, thinly sliced on the diagonal
3 ounces celery, thinly sliced on the diagonal
3 ounces broccoli, flowerettes divided into small pieces, stem thinly
    sliced on the diagonal
2 ounces asparagus, thinly sliced on the diagonal
1 small (3-ounce) zucchini, cut diagonally into ¼-inch ovals
2 ounces fresh shiitake or other mushroom, cut into ¼-inch slices
3 ounces snow peas, halved diagonally
6 tablespoons low-fat sour cream
Freshly ground black pepper
¼ cup snipped fresh chives

Bring a pot of water to a boil. Drop the pasta into the boiling water and cook for 4 minutes, or until barely done. Drain and set aside, reserving ½ cup liquid.

While the pasta is cooking, heat the oil in a wok or skillet. Add the shallots, garlic, and jalapeño pepper. Cook for about 2 minutes, or until soft. Add the carrot, celery, and broccoli stems. Cook for 1 minute. Add the asparagus, zucchini, shiitake, snow peas, and broccoli flowerettes along with ¼ cup reserved liquid. Cover and cook for 2 minutes. Add the remaining ¼ cup reserved liquid and cook a minute longer.

Add the drained pasta to the wok along with the sour cream and black pepper. Toss to mix, letting bits of sour cream show. Remove to a serving platter and sprinkle the chives on top.

Serves 4

◇Grilled Fillet of Trout with Oysters and Herb Sauce

The fresh herbs flavor the oysters, making a light sauce for the trout as well.

4 6-ounce trout fillets
Juice of 1½ lemons
2 tablespoons olive oil
Freshly ground black pepper
¼ cup dry white wine
1 clove garlic, smashed
1 sprig fresh tarragon, or 2 teaspoons dried tarragon
12 bluepoint oysters, shucked, liquid reserved
¼ cup chopped fresh parsley
¼ cup chopped fresh dill
1 jalapeño pepper, cored, seeded, and minced
2 teaspoons cornstarch dissolved in 2 teaspoons water
1 tablespoon corn oil
½ pound carrots, cut into ¼-inch rounds
½ pound zucchini, cut into ¼-inch rounds
1 tablespoon low-salt soy sauce

Place the trout in a flat bowl. Sprinkle the juice of one lemon, the olive oil, and black pepper on top. Turn to coat each fillet, then set aside to marinate for an hour.

Preheat an oiled grill until hot and the oven to 400° F.

Put the wine in a 1-quart pot with the garlic and tarragon. Simmer over medium heat until reduced to half. Discard the garlic and tarragon. Add the oysters and their liquid to the reduced wine along with the parsley, dill, and jalapeño pepper. Cook until the oysters begin to curl, about 2 minutes. Add the dissolved cornstarch and the juice of the remaining half lemon. Bring to a boil and cook until slightly thick. Set aside and keep warm.

Bring the corn oil and ¼ cup water to a boil in a saucepan. Add the carrots, cover, and cook until the water has been absorbed but the carrots are still crisp, about 5 minutes. Add the zucchini, cover again, and cook a few minutes longer. Season with black pepper and soy sauce. Keep warm until the fish is done.

Remove the trout fillets from the marinade and place them on the grill, skinned side down. Cook for 30 seconds to sear. Rotate each fillet 45 degrees and return to the grill, same side down, to sear with a diamond pattern. Carefully turn each fillet, seared side up, onto a baking pan and place in the oven for 3 to 4 minutes to finish cooking.

Place each trout fillet diagonally across a heated dinner plate. Spoon 3 oysters and their sauce on one side of the fish and the carrots and zucchini on the other side.

Serves 4

◇Tomato-Mozzarella Salad
◇Steamed Breast of Spring Chicken in Romaine

Instead of using lettuce in this vibrant insalata, I save it to wrap the chicken stuffed with wild rice. If you prepare the chicken for steaming early in the day, make the salad without the dressing, and cut the carrots and scallions, ahead, you can spend more time with your guests than in the kitchen.

Tomato-Mozzarella Salad   CAL 228

Pro 11.3 g, Cho 14.4 g, Fat 14.2 g, Sat 5.4 g, Chol 28.1 mg, Fiber 2.1 g, Ca 340.4 mg, Zn 2.1 mg, Fe 3.8 mg, Folate 76 mcg, Na 22.4 mg, Suc 0.2 g

Steamed Breast of Spring Chicken in Romaine   CAL 404

Pro 39.2 g, Cho 24.6 g, Fat 5.6 g, Sat 1.8 g, Chol 81.9 mg, Fiber 2.7 g, Ca 212.8 mg, Zn 3.4 mg, Fe 7.1 mg, Folate 306.3 mcg, Na 274.9 mg, Suc 2.4 g

Total Menu   CAL 632

Pro 50.5 g, Cho 39 g, Fat 19.8 g, Sat 7.2 g, Chol 110 mg, Fiber 4.8 g, Ca 553.2 mg, Zn 5.5 mg, Fe 10.9 mg, Folate 382.3 mcg, Na 297.3 mg, Suc 2.6 g

◇Tomato-Mozzarella Salad

In Italy, salads of tomato and fresh mozzarella di bufalo flavored with leaves of basil are a sure sign of summer. If you can't find mozzarella di bufalo, made from the milk of water buffalos, look for locally made soft unsalted mozzarella sold in Italian markets. Usually kept in water, it is so superior to the packaged supermarket varieties to be essentially a different cheese, and well worth the effort to obtain.

1 ounce piece red onion, thinly sliced

1½ pounds tomatoes, cored, not peeled, cut into 1-inch cubes

32 fresh basil leaves

1 small (¼-pound) cucumber or a ¼-pound section from a large (preferably hothouse) cucumber, halved, cut into ¼-inch slices

6 ounces unsalted mozzarella di bufalo, cut into ¾-inch cubes

¼ teaspoon freshly ground black pepper

2 tablespoons olive oil

1 tablespoon red wine vinegar

Place the red onion in a bowl of ice water for 10 to 15 minutes to crisp.

Divide the tomato cubes among 4 salad plates. Arrange the basil leaves, cucumbers, and cheese attractively on the plate. Drain the onions and sprinkle them on top. Grind black pepper on each plate. Mix together the oil and vinegar and drizzle it on top.

Serves 4

◇Steamed Breast of Spring Chicken in Romaine

Romaine lettuce makes a fine wrapping for foods. More fragile than cabbage, it imparts a delicate flavor while adding moisture.

4 5-ounce skinless, boneless chicken breasts
½ cup unflavored low-fat yogurt
½ teaspoon dried lemongrass (sereh)
½ teaspoon crushed red pepper flakes
½ teaspoon ground cumin
1 clove garlic, crushed
16 large romaine lettuce leaves
½ recipe Wild Rice (see below)
1 pound carrots, cut into ¼-inch rounds
4 scallions, sliced
2 cups Chicken Stock, reduced to ¾ cup
¼ cup chopped fresh chives

Place each chicken breast between 2 sheets of waxed paper and pound with the side of a meat pounder or heavy pot until about ¼ inch thick. Place the chicken in a baking dish and rub with the yogurt, lemongrass, red pepper flakes, cumin, and garlic. Cover and let marinate for 3 hours at room temperature or refrigerate overnight.

Bring a large pot of water to a boil. Choose large romaine leaves, avoiding the very hard outermost leaves. Drop them in the boiling water and cook just until soft, about 3 minutes. Drain, pat dry, and cut away the center ribs, leaving each leaf in 2 pieces.

Place the leaf halves, overlapping slightly, on a work surface in groups of 8 halves so they form rectangles about 9 inches wide and 8 inches long.

Remove the chicken from the marinade, wiping most of it off with your hands. Reserve the marinade. Place a chicken piece in the center of a bed of leaves. Spoon some of the wild rice across the center of the chicken so it goes in the same direction as the leaves.

Fold the breast over to enclose the stuffing, then wrap everything neatly in the romaine leaves. Place each package on a 14-inch sheet of good-quality plastic wrap. Fold the bottom tightly over; fold in the sides and roll up like an egg roll. This is easiest if you have someone to help who can keep the plastic taut as you work. Wrap with a second sheet of plastic in the opposite direction. Repeat with the remaining chicken, wild rice, and lettuce.

Bring some water or the liquid you used to blanch the lettuce to a boil in the bottom of a steamer or wok. Place the chicken rolls and carrots on a steamer rack over the boiling liquid. Cover and cook for 15 minutes. Remove the chicken to a plate, leaving the carrots in the steamer. Place something under part of the plate so it sits at an angle.

Add the scallions to the carrots in the steamer. Cover tightly and leave over the hot water, heat turned off. They will cook enough while you finish with the chicken and sauce.

With scissors, snip a small hole in each chicken package so the excess liquid runs out. Catch the liquid and add it to the chicken stock along with the reserved marinade. Cook over moderate heat just until heated through. Stir in the chives.

Cut the plastic wrap away from each chicken roll, Slice the very tip off one end of each roll to expose the stuffing. Then slice each roll on the diagonal into 4 or 5 pieces. Arrange them overlapping on individual plates. Spoon some of the sauce on top. Serve with the steamed carrots and scallions.

Serves 4

◇Wild Rice

Used as a stuffing for the chicken, the wild rice also is an excellent side dish with all kinds of meat and poultry dishes.

1 tablespoon sesame oil
½ cup (2 ounces) chopped onion
1 large (2-ounce) stalk celery, chopped
½ teaspoon minced garlic
½ teaspoon minced jalapeño pepper
¼ pound wild rice
1 bay leaf
2 tablespoons (½ ounce) toasted pine nuts (pignoli)
2 cups Chicken Stock

Heat the sesame oil in a 1½-quart pot. Add the onion, celery, garlic, and jalapeño pepper. Cook for 2 minutes, until lightly browned and soft. Add the remaining ingredients, bring to a boil, cover, and lower the heat so the liquid simmers. Continue cooking for 1¼ hours. Uncover and cook a few minutes longer until all the liquid has been absorbed. Discard the bay leaf.

Serves 4

◇Fish Mousse with Ragout of Wild Mushrooms and Peas
◇Breast of Chicken with Tomato and Vinegar

This is an elegant meal, starting with the pristine fish mousse garnished with the woodsy wild mushrooms and fresh peas. The seemingly more plebeian chicken belies its sophisticated seasoning.

Make the mousse mixture ahead and keep it refrigerated until ready for baking. You can also brown the chicken earlier, leaving it to finish cooking while you serve the first course.

Fish Mousse with Ragout of Wild Mushrooms and Peas   CAL 167

Pro 18.3 g, Cho 12.4 g, Fat 1.8 g, Sat 0.1 g, Chol 31.4 mg, Fiber 1.8 g, Ca 43 mg, Zn 1.3 mg, Fe 2.8 mg, Folate 76.1 mcg, Na 85.6 mg, Suc 1.4 g

Breast of Chicken with Tomato and Vinegar   CAL 432

Pro 35.8 g, Cho 40 g, Fat 8.2 g, Sat 1.4 g, Chol 74.4 mg, Fiber 1.1 g, Ca 56.3 mg, Zn 2.3 mg, Fe 4.7 mg, Folate 69.9 mcg, Na 143.8 mg, Suc 0.1 g

Total Menu   CAL 599

Pro 54.1 g, Cho 52.4 g, Fat 10 g, Sat 1.5 g, Chol 105.8 mg, Fiber 2.9 g, Ca 99.3 mg, Zn 3.6 mg, Fe 7.5 mg, Folate 146 mcg, Na 229.4 mg, Suc 1.5 g

◇Fish Mousse with Ragout of Wild Mushrooms and Peas

The mousse is a variation on fragile quenelles, made with egg whites and lots of heavy cream. While a bit denser than its richer relatives, this version has a delicacy of its own.

If you are cooking for eight, or want this as a main course, double the recipe and make it in a 6-cup ring mold. Cook in the water bath for 25 minutes.

½ teaspoon corn oil
¾ pound skinless striped bass or red snapper fillet
2 egg whites
Pinch ground cayenne pepper
1½ teaspoons brandy
¼ cup ice water
¼ cup dry vermouth
1 cup Chicken Stock, reduced to ¼ cup
½ pound mixed wild and button mushrooms, cut into chunks (if using shiitake, discard the stems)
½ cup scallions, cut into ½-inch pieces
2 sprigs fresh herbs (marjoram, thyme, tarragon)
½ jalapeño pepper, cored, seeded, and minced
1½ teaspoons arrowroot dissolved in 2 teaspoons cold water
½ pound peas, cooked for 2 minutes in boiling water

Preheat the oven to 325° F. Use the oil to grease four 1-cup ovenproof molds.

Put the fish through the fine blade of a meat grinder, then into the work bowl of a food processor with the egg whites, cayenne, and brandy. Process until smooth. If you don't have a meat grinder, mince the fish with a knife before putting it in the food processor. With the machine running, pour in the ice water and vermouth. The mixture should be very smooth.

Spoon the mixture into the prepared molds and smooth the tops. Place them in a larger baking pan. Add water to the pan so it comes halfway up the sides of the molds. Place the pan on top of the stove over medium heat and bring the water to a boil. Cover the pan and carefully transfer it to the oven. Cook for 12 to 15 minutes. Remove from the oven and let the molds rest, still covered.

Bring the reduced stock to a boil in a 2-quart pot. Add the mushrooms, scallions, herbs, and jalapeño pepper. Cook for 5 minutes. Stir in the dissolved arrowroot and simmer for 2 more minutes. (The sauce should be thick because the fish mousse will be giving off liquid that will slightly dilute the ragout.)

Loosen each fish mold all around with a flexible spatula. Place a salad plate over one mold. Flip the plate and mold together, giving them a firm shake to loosen the fish. Remove the mold, leaving the fish on the platter. Spoon some of the mushroom ragout on one side and the peas on the other. Repeat with the remaining molds and vegetables.

Serves 4

◇Breast of Chicken with Tomato and Vinegar

Jean Troisgros, one of the famous Troisgros brothers of Roanne, first created a tomato-vinegar sauce for chicken. This is one of the many variations I have evolved from his idea.

1 jalapeño pepper, cored, seeded, and minced

4 cloves garlic, minced

4 ¼-pound chicken breasts, all skin and fat removed, upper wings and bones still attached

Juice of 1 lemon

1 tablespoon olive oil

¼ cup red wine vinegar

1 teaspoon balsamic vinegar

¼ cup minced shallots

1 pound tomatoes, peeled, seeded, and chopped (2 cups)

Bouquet garni: 1 sprig fresh or 1 teaspoon dried rosemary, 1 tablespoon tarragon leaves or 1 teaspoon dried tarragon, and 1 bunch parsley stems

1 tablespoon tomato paste

½ cup Chicken Stock, water, or white wine

½ pound soba (Japanese buckwheat noodles)

Spread the jalapeño and garlic on the chicken along with the lemon juice. Set aside and let marinate for at least 2 hours.

Heat the oil in a 10-inch nonstick skillet. When it is hot, add the chicken pieces, skinned side down. Cook until browned, about 3 minutes. Turn and brown the other side, about 2 more minutes. Remove from the pan and pat dry. Pour out any fat in the pan.

Add the vinegars to the pan and scrape to loosen any thick bits on the bottom. Add the shallots, tomatoes, bouquet garni, tomato paste, and chicken stock. Stir to blend well. Place the chicken pieces on top. Partially cover and cook for about 5 minutes, or until the chicken is done and the sauce is thick.

While the chicken is cooking, drop the soba into a large pot of boiling water. Cook for 4 minutes, or until done. Drain and keep warm.

Serve the chicken with the tomato sauce and soba.

Serves 4

◇Baked Beefsteak Tomato with Goat Cheese and Corn
◇Breast of Chicken with Tomatillo Sauce

The red tomato stuffed with yellow corn and white cheese is followed by chicken breasts in a pale green tomato sauce, quite different in flavor and appearance. You can prepare the tomatoes ahead up to the actual baking. At the same time, make the tomatillo sauce and assemble the chicken.

Baked Beefsteak Tomato with Goat Cheese and Corn   CAL 232

Pro 10 g, Cho 29.6 g, Fat 10.4 g, Sat 4.7 g, Chol 25.1 mg, Fiber 3.1 g,
Ca 217.6 mg, Zn 1.7 mg, Fe 3.7 mg, Folate 163.4 mcg, Na 85.8 mg,
Suc 0.8 g

Breast of Chicken with Tomatillo Sauce   CAL 278

Pro 30.2 g, Cho 12.3 g, Fat 12 g, Sat 2.1 g, Chol 72.8 mg, Fiber 2.4 g,
Ca 49.1 mg, Zn 1.1 mg, Fe 2.9 mg, Folate 41.4 mcg, Na 88.3 mg,
Suc 0 g

Total Menu   CAL 510

Pro 40.2 g, Cho 41.9 g, Fat 22.4 g, Sat 6.8 g, Chol 97.9 mg, Fiber 5.5 g,
Ca 266.7 mg, Zn 2.8 mg, Fe 6.6 mg, Folate 204.8 mcg, Na 174.1 mg,
Suc 0.8 g

◇Baked Beefsteak Tomato with Goat Cheese and Corn

I also like to serve this hearty vegetarian first course as a main course for a summer lunch. It is only worth making when you can get full-flavored beefsteak tomatoes. Fill them ahead; bake just before serving.

4 large (12-ounce) tomatoes
Freshly ground black pepper
1 cup (¼ pound) corn cut from 2 medium ears or substitute frozen corn
1 tablespoon olive oil
1 medium (¼-pound) red onion, halved, cut into ¼-inch slices
1 green bell pepper, cored, seeded, and cut lengthwise into ½-inch strips
1 clove garlic, minced
2 tablespoons minced jalapeño pepper
⅓ cup roughly chopped fresh basil leaves
2 scallions, cut into ¼-inch rounds
¼ pound unsalted young goat cheese, cut into 4 even pieces

Preheat the oven to 400° F.

Core the tomatoes. Cut a slice about ¾ inch thick off the bottom of each. Save these slices to be the caps. With a spoon, scoop out and reserve most of the pulp, leaving the walls at least ¼ inch thick and the bottom at least ½ inch. Grind black pepper over the tomato shells and set aside.

If using fresh corn, bring a small pot of water to a boil. Add the corn and cook for 1 minute. Drain and reserve. If using frozen corn, just defrost and pat dry.

Heat the olive oil in a 10-inch ovenproof skillet. Add the onion, bell pepper, garlic, and 1 tablespoon jalapeño pepper. Cook over medium-high heat for 5 minutes, then add the tomato pulp. Cook for 3 minutes more. Remove from the heat.

Place the 4 tomatoes over the cooked mixture in the pan. Put a fourth of the basil in each tomato. Top it with a fourth of the corn, then a fourth of the scallions. Put a piece of goat cheese over that and sprinkle the remaining jalapeño pepper on top. Cap each tomato with a reserved slice.

Place in the preheated oven and bake for about 40 minutes. The caps of the tomatoes should be black, the cheese beginning to run down the sides. Pull the burnt skin off the cap of each tomato, but leave the skin on the sides of the shells. Serve the tomatoes on individual plates with some of the green pepper–tomato sauce spooned on top.

Serves 4

◇Breast of Chicken with Tomatillo Sauce

In Mexico, they cook with green tomatoes called tomatillos that are actually members of the gooseberry family. They are sold fresh throughout the Southwest and in specialty stores elsewhere. If you have tomatillos, peel off the papery husk and wash off the sticky residue before using. If they are not available, use true unripe green tomatoes rather than canned tomatillos.

2 tablespoons corn oil

2 tablespoons minced jalapeño pepper

1 teaspoon minced garlic

2 tablespoons minced shallots

½ pound tomatillos, cut into ¼-inch chunks (about 1 cup)

2 tablespoons chopped cilantro (fresh coriander)

⅛ teaspoon ground cumin

2 tablespoons (½ ounce) petitas (green pumpkin seeds)

¼ cup Chicken Stock

Freshly ground black pepper

4 ¼-pound boneless, skinless chicken breasts

1 5-ounce red bell pepper, cored, seeded, and cut into julienne strips

1 5-ounce green bell pepper, cored, seeded, and cut into julienne strips

1 5-ounce yellow bell pepper, cored, seeded, and cut into julienne strips

Heat 1 tablespoon corn oil in an 8-inch skillet. Add half the jalapeño pepper, the garlic, and shallots. Cook for about 3 minutes to soften. Add the tomatillos, chopped cilantro, and cumin. Cover and cook for about 20 minutes, or until everything is very soft.

Let the mixture cool a bit, then puree it with the pepitas in a blender or food processor (blender preferred) until pale green, creamy, and smooth. Add the chicken stock and puree some more.

Preheat the oven to 350° F. Grind black pepper on each chicken piece.

Spoon some sauce into an 8-inch pie plate or other baking dish that will just hold the chicken in a single layer. Arrange the chicken, skinned side up, over the sauce. Pour the remaining sauce on top. Bake for 20 minutes.

Shortly before the chicken is done, heat the remaining 1 tablespoon oil in an 8-inch skillet. Add the remaining jalapeño pepper, the bell peppers, and a bit of water to make some steam. Cook, stirring often, for 5 minutes, or until the peppers are soft.

Arrange a chicken breast with some sauce on each of 4 plates. Garnish each with some of the sautéed peppers.

Serves 4

◇Cold Paupiettes of Trout with Red Pepper Mousse
◇Breast of Chicken with Winter Vegetables in Papillote

The cold trout rolls with their herbaceous sauce whet the appetite for the chicken served in its intriguing package. Almost everything can be done ahead. Put the papillotes in the oven when you serve the fish.

Cold Paupiettes of Trout with Red Pepper Mousse   CAL 303

Pro 22.8 g, Cho 19.7 g, Fat 14.6 g, Sat 3.2 g, Chol 47.4 mg, Fiber 1.6 g, Ca 95.1 mg, Zn 1.7 mg, Fe 3.2 mg, Folate 58.6 mcg, Na 96.7 mg, Suc 0.7 g

Breast of Chicken with Winter Vegetables in Papillote   CAL 307

Pro 28.8 g, Cho 19.5 g, Fat 10.1 g, Sat 1.7 g, Chol 66.1 mg, Fiber 3.5 g, Ca 95.6 mg, Zn 2.8 mg, Fe 4.2 mg, Folate 54.9 mcg, Na 252.5 mg, Suc 1.2 g

Total Menu   CAL 610

Pro 51.6 g, Cho 39.2 g, Fat 24.7 g, Sat 4.9 g, Chol 113.5 mg, Fiber 5.1 g, Ca 190.7 mg, Zn 4.5 mg, Fe 7.4 mg, Folate 113.5 mcg, Na 349.2 mg, Suc 1.9 g

◇Cold Paupiettes of Trout with Red Pepper Mousse

Although we serve everything on white plates at The Four Seasons, this dish, with its red bull's-eye surrounded by white fish on a pool of green sauce would look wonderful on black.

Freshly ground white pepper
4 3-ounce skinless trout fillets
Juice of ½ lemon
2 tablespoons dry white wine
1 tablespoon plus ½ teaspoon olive oil
½ recipe Red Pepper Puree Sauce (see page 28)
¾ teaspoon unflavored gelatin dissolved in 1 tablespoon water
1 teaspoon finely chopped jalapeño pepper
Vegetable Stock or water
2 ounces soba (Japanese buckwheat noodles)
½ 2.5-ounce package 2-Mamina (Japanese radish sprouts)
1½ teaspoons red wine vinegar
½ cup Green Herb Sauce (see below)
½ pound cucumbers, cut into rounds
½ bunch fresh dill
2 ounces daikon (Japanese radish), grated

Grind white pepper on the trout fillets. Mix together the lemon juice and white wine in a shallow bowl. Add the trout and let it marinate for 30 minutes. Drain.

Preheat the oven to 350° F.

Brush four ½-cup ovenproof ramekins with the ½ teaspoon olive oil. Coil the fillets, skinned side in, so they fit into the ramekins. The center will be empty. Bake in the oven for 10 minutes. Set aside on a rack to cool.

Heat the red pepper puree sauce until it is bubbly. Stir in the dissolved gelatin and jalapeño pepper. Make sure the gelatin is spread evenly throughout. Spoon the sauce into the centers of the ramekins, dividing it evenly. Refrigerate until set.

Meanwhile, bring vegetable stock or water to a boil. Add the soba and cook until barely done, about 4 minutes. Drain, rinse, and chill. Mix the noodles with the 2-Mamina, remaining tablespoon olive oil, and vinegar.

Spoon some green herb sauce into the center of each of 4 plates. Run a knife around the inside edge of each ramekin to loosen the fish, then turn them out, one at a time, into your hand. Place them, one per plate, top side up, over the sauce. Garnish with the buckwheat noodles and cucumber slices, dill, and grated daikon.

Serves 4

◇Green Herb Sauce

This makes more than you will need for the trout recipe. However, it will last for a while and makes an excellent sauce for grilled fish.

½ cup fresh parsley
½ cup fresh spinach leaves
½ cup 2-Mamina (Japanese radish sprouts)
½ cup watercress leaves
½ cup (2 ounces) minced shallots
1 clove garlic, minced
2 teaspoons salt-free mustard
Juice of 1 lemon
½ cup Fish Stock
½ cup olive oil
¼ teaspoon freshly ground black pepper
1 jalapeño pepper, cored and seeded

Bring a pot of water to a boil. Add the parsley and cook for 30 seconds. Drain well and squeeze dry. Add the spinach, 2-Mamina, and watercress, cooking them for 1 minute. Drain well and squeeze dry.

Put all the blanched greens in a food processor or blender with the other ingredients. Run until pureed, then press through the fine disk of a food mill.

Makes 2 cups

◇Breast of Chicken with Winter Vegetables in Papillote

Heart-shaped paper makes an attractive way to cook fish or chicken with vegetables. It steams everything together, mixing the flavors of the foods, and makes an impressive presentation. Don't let the egg in the ingredients throw you off. It's not for eating, but just to seal the packages.

3 dried red chili peppers
Rind of ½ lime
2 bay leaves
1½ teaspoons mace
4 ¼-pound skinless, boneless chicken breast halves
1 clove garlic
3 ounces peeled carrot, cut into 8 turned (see page 20) 1½- to 2-inch pieces
3 ounces peeled kohlrabi, cut into 8 turned 1½- to 2-inch pieces
8 ½-ounce pearl onions, peeled
3 ounces peeled turnip, cut into 8 turned 1½- to 2-inch pieces
3 ounces peeled parsnip, cut into 8 turned 1½- to 2-inch pieces
5 ounces ramps or leeks, cut diagonally into ¼-inch slices
2 cups Chicken Stock, reduced to ¼ cup
1 tablespoon plus 1 teaspoon olive oil
1 egg (for sealing the packages)

Put 2 red peppers, the lime rind, bay leaves, and mace in a spice or coffee grinder. Grind until the mixture is very fine. Coat the chicken with the spice mixture. Set aside to marinate for 2 to 3 hours.

Bring a pot of water to a boil with the remaining red pepper and the garlic. Add the carrot, kohlrabi, and onions. Cook for 20 minutes, or until barely done. Set the vegetables aside, discarding the garlic and pepper. In the same liquid, cook the turnips and parsnips for 10 minutes, or until barely done. Set aside with the other vegetables. Still using the same liquid, cook the ramps or leeks for 2 minutes; drain and discard the liquid. Leave the ramps in the pot. Add the reduced stock and toss over heat to coat. Set aside.

Heat 1 tablespoon oil in a 10-inch nonstick pan. Put the chicken in it, skinned side down. Cook over medium-high heat for 2 minutes and turn and cook 1 minute on the other side—a total of 3 minutes. The chicken will finish cooking in the oven.

Take 4 sheets of parchment paper, each about 13 inches square. Fold them in half and cut along the open sides to make half a heart. (When you open them, you will have full hearts.) Dribble ½ teaspoon oil on one sheet, top with another, and rub them together to give each sheet a light coating of oil. Repeat with the other 2 sheets of parchment and remaining oil.

Working with one sheet at a time, place it, oiled side up, on your work surface. Put one chicken breast to one side of the crease. Arrange two of each turned vegetable and two onions around the edge. Spoon a fourth of the ramps with a bit of their liquid on top of the chicken. Beat the egg in a small bowl. With a pastry brush, paint a thick line of egg around the edge of the heart. Fold the paper over and press the edges together. Brush more egg along the cut edge. Starting at the indentation of the heart, crimp and fold the paper over to make an attractive and tight seal. Work in this way around the complete cut edge. Fold the end bit under. Repeat with the remaining paper and ingredients.

You can make the packages in the morning and refrigerate them. Be sure to bring them to room temperature before cooking. Adjust the racks in your oven so there is enough space between them and between the top rack and the top of the oven for the packages to puff up. Preheat the oven to 475° F. Put the packages on baking sheets. Two should fit on each sheet. Bake for 6 minutes. The packages should puff up. Place each on a heated dinner plate and serve immediately or the packages will start to deflate.

Serves 4

◇Shrimp and Vegetables à la Grecque
◇Roasted Peppers, Buckwheat Noodles, and Chicken Salad

Although both these dishes can be called salads, they are quite different in style. An ethnic mélange, the shrimp and vegetables, with their Greek flavoring, are served over American wild rice. For the chicken salad, the Italian roasted peppers are mixed with Japanese soba. As is often true of my menus, most of the work can be done ahead. The vegetables for the first course do not require much attention once they are cut up. Should you prefer, cook them ahead and either serve at room temperature or re-heat briefly. The chicken salad only gets better if it sits for a few hours.

Shrimp and Vegetables à la Grecque
CAL 223

Pro 15.6 g, Cho 23.4 g, Fat 7.1 g, Sat 0.7 g, Chol 51.1 mg, Fiber 2 g, Ca 89.6 mg, Zn 3.3 mg, Fe 4.5 mg, Folate 89.1 mcg, Na 166.3 mg, Suc 1.1 g

Roasted Peppers, Buckwheat Noodles, and Chicken Salad   CAL 463

Pro 31.8 g, Cho 63.4 g, Fat 11.2 g, Sat 1.6 g, Chol 55.7 mg, Fiber 6.7 g, Ca 194.8 mg, Zn 2.4 mg, Fe 7 mg, Folate 125.5 mcg, Na 150.1 mg, Suc 0 g

Total Menu   CAL 686

Pro 47.4 g, Cho 86.8 g, Fat 18.3 g, Sat 2.3 g, Chol 106.8 mg, Fiber 8.7 g, Ca 284.4 mg, Zn 5.7 mg, Fe 11.5 mg, Folate 214.6 mcg, Na 316.4 mg, Suc 1.1 g

◇Shrimp and Vegetables à la Grecque

Cooked vegetable salads like this one are generally attributed to the Greeks. By adding the shrimp, I've turned this into a course rather than a side dish. Vary the greens with the market. Arugula, Bibb lettuce, or mâche would be equally good.

2 cups water
1 dried red chili pepper
¼ pound cauliflower, separated into flowerettes
¼ pound carrot, cut into 1-inch chunks
¼ pound fennel, cut into 1-inch squares
1 small (4-ounce) onion, cut into 1-inch chunks
2 cloves garlic, minced
1 teaspoon saffron threads
½ green bell pepper, cored, seeded, and cut into 1-inch squares
¼ pound button mushrooms
1 tablespoon olive oil
½ pound shelled, deveined shrimp
1 head Boston lettuce
½ recipe Wild Rice (see page 90)
¼ cup chopped fresh Italian parsley

Bring the water and chili pepper to a boil in a 3-quart saucepan. Add the cauliflower, carrot, fennel, onion, garlic, and saffron. Cook for 10 minutes. Add the bell pepper, mushrooms, and olive oil. Cook 5 minutes longer, or until almost all the liquid has been absorbed. Add the shrimp and cook 2 minutes more. The liquid should be gone; the shrimp, just cooked.

To serve, spread the Boston lettuce on a platter. Spoon the wild rice in the center. Top with the shrimp and vegetables. Sprinkle the Italian parsley on top.

Serves 4

◇Roasted Peppers, Buckwheat Noodles, and Chicken Salad

This is an attractive and filling salad to serve at room temperature. It looks a bit complicated at first, but the only really time-consuming part is roasting the peppers. Not only can they be done the night before, they will be better if they are.

ROASTED PEPPERS

3 6-ounce red bell peppers
3 6-ounce yellow bell peppers
Freshly ground black pepper
1 tablespoon olive oil
1 clove garlic, minced
2 tablespoons minced jalapeño pepper
½ cup thinly sliced shallots
1 packed teaspoon fresh oregano leaves, halved, or ¼ teaspoon dried oregano
2 tablespoons red wine vinegar

Heat a grill or broiler until hot. Put the bell peppers directly on the grill or on a rack close to the broiler. Cook, turning with tongs as needed, until the skins are black all over. Remove from the heat. While they are still warm, but cooled enough to handle, peel away and discard the skin with a paring knife or your fingers. Cut the peppers in half and remove and discard the cores and seeds. If necessary, rinse them in a little water. The less water, the better. It cuts down on the flavor of the peppers. Cut each half lengthwise into strips 1 inch wide. Place them on a plate and grind fresh black pepper on top.

Heat the olive oil in a 6-inch skillet. Add the garlic, jalapeño pepper, shallots, and oregano. Cook over high heat for 1 to 2 minutes, until the shallots and garlic are lightly browned. Remove the pan from the heat and stir in the vinegar. Scrape the pan with a wooden spoon to deglaze. Pour the seasonings over the peppers. Cover with plastic wrap and marinate at least 2 hours. You can do these the day ahead. (These are the Roasted Peppers used in other recipes.)

SALAD

1 generous cup (2 ounces) watercress
2 6-ounce boneless, skinless chicken breasts
6 ounces cha soba (Japanese green tea buckwheat noodles)
1 pound tomatoes, peeled, cored, seeded, and cut into 1-inch chunks
½ pound zucchini, cut into julienne strips
1 tablespoon red wine vinegar
1 tablespoon olive oil
1 teaspoon low-salt soy sauce
Freshly ground black pepper
Roasted Peppers
¼ cup fresh basil leaves or 2-Mamina (Japanese radish sprouts)
4 white mushroom caps, thinly sliced, or 1 100-gram (3.5-ounce) package enoki mushrooms

Fill a 3-quart pot with water and bring it to a boil.

Place the watercress in a deep strainer. Place it over the pot with boiling water so the watercress is submerged. Leave for about 45 seconds. If necessary, spoon some of the boiling water over the watercress so it all cooks. Rinse quickly under cold water to stop the cooking. Squeeze dry with your hands, then roughly chop. Set aside.

Cut the chicken on the diagonal into thin strips. Place it in the same strainer and cook in the boiling water for 10 seconds the same way you cooked the watercress. Rinse briefly in the cold water to stop the cooking, then put aside with the watercress.

Drop the soba in the same boiling water and cook until done, about 4 minutes. Drain and rinse under cold water.

Toss together the soba, chicken, tomatoes, watercress, zucchini, vinegar, olive oil, soy sauce, and freshly ground pepper. Transfer to a round platter or shallow bowl. Arrange the peppers alternating around the pasta. Spoon any extra shallots or liquid on top. Garnish with the basil and mushrooms.

Serves 4

ROASTED PEPPERS, BUCKWHEAT NOODLES, AND CHICKEN SALAD

◇Borscht
◇Oriental Steamed Chicken and Ham

Here is a blending of eastern Europe and the Far East. The borscht is best cooked the day ahead and reheated. You can prepare the chicken and ham packages ahead as well, ready for steaming.

Borscht   CAL 277

Pro 17.4 g, Cho 24.8 g, Fat 8.2 g, Sat 3.3 g, Chol 40 mg, Fiber 2 g,
Ca 89.3 mg, Zn 5.2 mg, Fe 4.3 mg, Folate 144.6 mcg, Na 147.7 mg,
Suc 0.6 g

Oriental Steamed Chicken and Ham
CAL 328

Pro 33.5 g, Cho 39.7 g, Fat 4.7 g, Sat 1.1 g, Chol 69.3 mg, Fiber 2.6 g,
Ca 137 mg, Zn 1.8 mg, Fe 2.7 mg, Folate 98.5 mcg, Na 502.2 mg,
Suc 0 g

Total Menu   CAL 605

Pro 50.9 g, Cho 64.5 g, Fat 12.9 g, Sat 4.4 g, Chol 109.3 mg, Fiber 4.6 g,
Ca 226.3 mg, Zn 7 mg, Fe 7 mg, Folate 243.1 mcg, Na 649.9 mg,
Suc 0.6 g

◇Borscht

This traditional Russian Jewish soup is made hot with meat, cold without. Most often, it is sweet and sour. Some people try to get the effect with artificial sweeteners, but I never use them. I prefer to use a little real sugar. However, in this version the flavor of the beets is enhanced by a little horseradish. It more than makes up for the sugar.

½ pound beef brisket, trimmed of all fat

3 cups Chicken Stock or water

1 bay leaf

½ teaspoon corn oil

1 small (3-ounce) onion, minced

1 jalapeño pepper, cored, seeded, and minced

1 clove garlic, minced

2 tablespoons red wine vinegar

1 pound beets (weighed with the leaves on), peeled and cut into
   julienne strips (by hand or with a food processor)

1 small (1½-ounce) turnip, peeled and cut into julienne strips

6 ounces potato, peeled and cut into ½-inch cubes

½ teaspoon caraway seed

¼ pound tomatoes, peeled, cored, seeded, and chopped

¼ pound cabbage, halved, cut crosswise into ¼-inch strips

1½ teaspoons prepared or freshly grated horseradish

¼ cup low-fat sour cream

4 teaspoons chopped fresh dill

Put the brisket in a pot with the stock and bay leaf. Bring to a boil, then lower the heat and simmer, partially covered, until very soft. This can take up to 3 hours. Check the pot from time to time to be sure the liquid hasn't reduced too much and add more as needed. When the meat is done, set it aside. Remove all the fat from the stock and measure it. You need 2 cups. If you have less, add water. If you have more, cook over high heat until reduced to 2 cups.

Heat the oil in a clean 2-quart soup pot. Add the onion, jalapeño pepper, and garlic. Cook until the vegetables are light brown. Add the vinegar and scrape the bottom of the pan to deglaze. Add the beets, turnip, potato, caraway seeds, and reserved stock. Bring to a boil, lower the heat to a simmer, and cook, partially covered, for 1½ hours. Add the tomatoes, cabbage, and horseradish and cook 15 minutes longer.

To serve, dice the brisket and add it to the soup to reheat. Top each serving with sour cream and a sprinkling of dill.

Serves 4

◇Oriental Steamed Chicken and Ham

There is a mysterious quality to dishes like this because all the ingredients are hidden in paper. I especially like this one because the chicken and ham go so well together.

4 scallions, cut diagonally into 2-inch pieces

2½ ounces carrot, cut into very thin strips

¾ pound boneless, skinless chicken breast, cut into 16 even slices

¼ pound lean smoked ham, cut into 12 ⅛-inch slices

2 tablespoons minced fresh ginger

Freshly ground black pepper

1 teaspoon low-salt soy sauce

2 eggs (for sealing the packages)

1½ pounds snow peas

¼ pound fresh spinach fettuccine

Bring a pot of water to a boil.

Have four 14-x-16-inch sheets of parchment paper on your work surface with the shorter ends facing you. Mix the scallions and carrot strips together, then divide them into 16 piles. Take one parchment sheet and place a piece of chicken about 3 inches in from the right edge. Arrange a pile of scallion and carrot on top of it, slightly overlapping to the left. Next slightly overlap a piece of ham, another piece of chicken, more scallion and carrot, ham, chicken, vegetables, ham, vegetables, chicken. Sprinkle a fourth of the ginger on top and grind on some black pepper. Sprinkle ¼ teaspoon soy sauce over everything.

With a pastry brush, paint egg generously around the edge of the paper. Fold up the bottom third to cover the chicken and ham. Brush more egg around the new edge. Fold in the sides and press to seal. Fold the top over and seal with more egg. The package should be secure but not too tight. Mark it somehow to indicate which is the top and which is the left side. Make 3 more packages with the remaining ingredients.

Bring water to a boil in the bottom of a steamer or wok. Place the packages on a steamer rack, cover, and place over the boiling water to steam for 8 minutes. Remove from the steamer and let rest a moment while you steam the snow peas for 3 minutes. At the same time, boil the fettuccine for 4 minutes, or until barely done.

Drain the fettuccine and divide it among 4 dinner plates. Cut open the marked left sides of the packages. Carefully slide out the chicken and ham on top of the fettuccine so each portion keeps its shape. Serve the snow peas on the side.

Serves 4

NOTE: If you don't have parchment paper, waxed paper is a satisfactory substitute.

◇Chayote Stuffed with Crabmeat
◇Stir-fried Chicken and Broccoli

The chayote stuffed with crabmeat is some-what oriental in feeling, a fine introduction to the chicken and broccoli, cooked in the Chinese style. Like most of these dishes, the chayotes can be prepared ahead, baked just before serving, The chicken, however, is best stir-fried at the last minute.

Chayote Stuffed with Crabmeat   CAL 158

Pro 12.3 g, Cho 18.4 g, Fat 5 g, Sat 2.7 g, Chol 37.6 mg, Fiber 2.2 g, Ca 55.2 mg, Zn 1.5 mg, Fe 1.9 mg, Folate 70.4 mcg, Na 16.3 g, Suc 0 g

Stir-fried Chicken and Broccoli   CAL 276

Pro 32.2 g, Cho 11 g, Fat 11.9 g, Sat 1.3 g, Chol 72.3 mg, Fiber 2.4 g, Ca 88.4 mg, Zn 1.6 mg, Fe 2.4 mg, Folate 77 mcg, Na 147.4 mg, Suc 0.1 g

Total Menu   CAL 434

Pro 44.5 g, Cho 29.4 g, Fat 16.9 g, Sat 4 g, Chol 109.9 mg, Fiber 4.6 g, Ca 143.6 mg, Zn 3.1 mg, Fe 4.3 mg, Folate 147.4 mcg, Na 163.7 mg, Suc 0.1 g

◇Chayote Stuffed with Crabmeat

Chayotes are pale green pear-shaped vegetables in the squash family. Also called mirlitons, they are commonly used in South American and Cajun cooking, but little known in most of this country. The taste is mild; the thin skin hides very pale flesh and a flat, soft pit.

2 chayotes (mirlitons)
1 tablespoon corn oil
1 clove garlic, minced
1 jalapeño pepper, cored, seeded, and minced
½ green bell pepper, cored, seeded, and cut into ¼-inch squares
    (¾ cup)
½ red bell pepper, cored, seeded, and cut into ¼-inch squares
    (¾ cup)
½ yellow bell pepper, cored, seeded, and cut into ¼-inch squares
    (¾ cup)
1 ¼-pound tomato, peeled, cored, seeded, and cut into ¼-inch
    cubes
½ cup (2 ounces) corn cut from 1 medium ear or substitute frozen
    corn, defrosted
1 tablespoon cilantro (fresh coriander)
½ pound crabmeat (lump, Alaska king, stone)
1 tablespoon Chicken or Vegetable Stock or water

Preheat the oven to 350° F.

Peel the chayotes and cut them in half through the natural indentation in the sides. Cut a small piece off the curved end of each half so it can lie flat on a plate. Cut out and discard the pit. With a melon baller, remove enough flesh from each half to make a shell about ½ inch thick on the sides and bottoms. Save the trimmings.

Heat the oil in an 8-inch skillet. Add the garlic and jalapeño pepper. Cook for 1 minute, then add the bell peppers and tomato along with the chayote trimmings. Cook for about 2 minutes. Put the mixture into a bowl. Add the corn, cilantro, and crabmeat. Mix well.

Place the chayote shells in a 10-inch pie plate so the smaller ends meet in the middle. Divide the crabmeat mixture among the shells, mounding up the filling. Put any extra filling in the center of the plate where the shells meet. Pour the stock or water into the plate's bottom. Cover with aluminum foil to seal and bake for 20 minutes. Open the foil and spoon any liquid in the plate over the stuffing. Bake 25 minutes longer, or until soft all the way through.

Serves 4

◇Stir-fried Chicken and Broccoli

Stir-frying, a basic Chinese technique, allows food to cook quickly so it retains its shape, color, and texture.

4 ¼-pound skinless, boneless chicken breasts, cut diagonally into
    ½-inch slices
1 teaspoon ground Szechuan peppercorns
2 tablespoons peanut or sesame oil
1 clove garlic
1 jalapeño pepper, cored, seeded, and cut into julienne strips
2 tablespoons julienned peeled ginger
1 large (2-ounce) stalk celery, cut diagonally into ¼-inch pieces
3 ounces Chinese cabbage, cut into 1-inch squares
1 large scallion, cut diagonally into ¼-inch pieces
1 medium red bell pepper, peeled, cored, seeded, and cut into
    ½-inch squares
¼ pound cucumber, cut into ¾-inch cubes
3 ounces soybean sprouts
1 cup sliced mushrooms (any kind)
5 ounces broccoli flowerettes, blanched in boiling water for 1 minute
1 teaspoon low-salt soy sauce
2 teaspoons arrowroot dissolved in ¼ cup Chicken Stock or water

Toss the chicken with the Szechuan pepper.

Heat the oil in a wok over high heat. Add the garlic, jalapeño pepper, ginger, and chicken. Cook for about 2 minutes, until the chicken is slightly brown, no longer raw. Remove everything to a bowl.

Add the vegetables to the wok along with ¼ cup water. The water creates steam to cook everything faster. Cook for about 4 minutes.

Return the chicken and seasonings to the wok. Add the soy sauce. Stir the stock-arrowroot mixture and add to the wok. Gently stir everything to coat. If the sauce seems watery, push the vegetables to the sides and let the sauce boil for 2 to 3 minutes in the bottom to thicken.

Serves 4

◇Vegetable Roll with Gado-Gado
◇Shrimp and Chicken Skewer

This meal is, in many ways, typical of me. The gado-gado sauce is one I learned from my Indonesian wife. I started making skewers when I was at La Fonda del Sol. It was the first time I used shrimp in that way. Now, the shrimp and chipolote skewer is a popular dish in the Bar Room.

The vegetable roll, while time-consuming to make, is beautiful to look at and delicious to eat. Fortunately, you can assemble it early in the day. You can even prepare the vegetables the day before, marinating the shrimp at the same time. Assemble the skewers and make the gado-gado before your guests arrive. The final attended cooking time will be brief.

Vegetable Roll with Gado-Gado   CAL 191

Pro 9.1 g, Cho 16.1 g, Fat 10.9 g, Sat 2.1 g, Chol 3.4 g, Fiber 2.2 g, Ca 144.8 mg, Zn 2.4 mg, Fe 1.9 mg, Folate 51.4 mcg, Na 303.4 mg, Suc 0 g

Shrimp and Chicken Skewer   CAL 414

Pro 33.8 g, Cho 39 g, Fat 11.7 g, Sat 1.4 g, Chol 100.3 mg, Fiber 3.1 g, Ca 102.6 mg, Zn 4.6 mg, Fe 5.8 mg, Folate 96.6 mcg, Na 206.6 mg, Suc 0.5 g

Total Menu   CAL 605

Pro 42.9 g, Cho 55.1 g, Fat 22.6 g, Sat 3.5 g, Chol 103.7 mg, Fiber 5.3 g, Ca 247.4 mg, Zn 7 mg, Fe 7.7 mg, Folate 148 mcg, Na 510 mg, Suc 0.5 g

◇Vegetable Roll with Gado-Gado

The inspiration for this vegetable roll comes from Japanese rolled sushi dishes. Rather than black nori (seaweed), the roll is encased in blanched greens, leeks in this case. Other vegetables and combinations will work as well, including spinach, chard, scallions, string beans, and tomatoes. Try to vary colors and shape. The more even your pieces, the more attractive the result. However, there is no need to be perfect. As long as there is variety in color and shape, each slice will look beautiful.

1 ounce oriental eggplant
1 ounce zucchini
1 ounce carrot
2 ounces green cabbage
1 ounce leek
1 ounce thin asparagus or scallions
1 ounce tofu, cut into ¼-inch cubes
1 ounce alfalfa sprouts
2 ounces red, yellow, and green bell peppers, cut into ¼-inch-wide
  strips
Gado-Gado (see below)

If you have a mandoline (a slicing tool), use it here to make even, paper-thin slices of eggplant, zucchini, and carrot. Trim the ends off all of them, but peel only the carrot. Cut the strips lengthwise, making them as long as the vegetable.

Bring a pot of water to a boil. Cut the thick cores from the cabbage leaves and discard, leaving each leaf in 2 pieces. Cut the leek in half through the root. Drop the leek and cabbage into the boiling water and cook until soft, about 5 minutes. Drain and pat dry. Cut the root off the leek and separate the leaves. Lay them flat in a pile. In the same water, cook the asparagus or scallions until just done.

It is easiest to make the roll on a bamboo sushi mat, sold in oriental shops. They are about 9½ inches square. If a mat is not available, work on a damp dish towel, napkin, or several layers of cheesecloth.

Place the mat on your work surface so the bamboo slats run sideways. Arrange the eggplant strips on it in a layer, slightly overlapping, so they extend up and down. Do not worry about them being exactly even. Next spread the tofu over the eggplant. Top this with alfalfa sprouts, covering the bottom two thirds of the tofu. Arrange the bell pepper strips on top, running from left to right so they cover the sprouts in a single layer. Starting with the bottom of the mat, tightly roll up the vegetables into a cylinder. Squeeze it hard to eliminate excess liquid. Peel away the mat and set the roll aside.

Return the mat to the work surface. Cover the mat with leek strips, placing them up and down with the white parts on the bottom. Follow with a layer of carrots, also going up and down. Next cover the carrots with the blanched cabbage leaves. Over that, put the asparagus spears, running across the cabbage, followed by zucchini. Spread the remaining sprouts over the upper third of the zucchini and the remaining tofu over the rest.

Put the eggplant-encased roll over the tofu. Once again, roll up the vegetables, with the first roll inside. Squeeze to eliminate any liquid. Wrap tightly in several layers of plastic wrap. Refrigerate until ready to cook.

Bring water to a boil in the bottom of a steamer or wok. Place the roll on the steamer basket. Cover and steam for 5 to 6 minutes. Remove from the steamer and place on a plate that is raised at one end. Pierce the plastic in several places to let the excess liquid run out. Let the roll rest a few minutes while you make the peanut sauce.

Trim the ends of the roll so they are even. Then cut it into 8 even rounds. Serve each person 2 rounds with some of the gado-gado.

Serves 4

◇Gado-Gado

In Indonesia and Africa, ground peanuts are often used in sauces. I've lightened the typical gado-gado by using yogurt instead of milk.

1½ teaspoons sesame oil
⅓ cup minced shallots
1 clove garlic, minced
1 teaspoon chopped fresh lemongrass, or ¼ teaspoon dried
    lemongrass (sereh)
1 teaspoon ulek sambal (Indonesian chili paste)
1½ tablespoons ketjap manis (Indonesian soy sauce)
1½ teaspoons grated fresh ginger
½ teaspoon ground cumin
½ teaspoon ground coriander
2 ounces (¼ cup) unsalted peanut butter
1 cup unflavored low-fat yogurt

Heat the oil in a saucepan. Add the shallots, garlic, lemongrass, and sambal. Cook over medium heat until lightly brown.

Stir in the ketjap, ginger, cumin, and coriander. Once smooth, add the peanut butter. Whisk until smooth. Whisk in the yogurt and continue cooking until the sauce thickens enough to coat a spoon.

Makes about 1½ cups

◇Shrimp and Chicken Skewer

We always have at least one skewer on the Bar Room lunch menu. This is a pretty and delicious version.

1 jalapeño pepper, cored, seeded, and minced
2 tablespoons minced shallot plus 1 large shallot, sliced
¼ cup chopped fresh parsley
Rind of ½ lemon, minced
4 cloves garlic, minced
12 large peeled, deveined shrimp (10 ounces)
½ pound skinless, boneless chicken breast, cut into 12 ½-inch strips
Juice of 1 lemon
1 tablespoon olive oil
1 teaspoon crumbled dried red chili pepper
10 fresh basil leaves, minced
10 fresh mint leaves, minced
1½ pounds tomatoes, peeled, cored, seeded, and cut into 1-inch chunks
1 recipe Wild Rice (see page 90)

Chop together the jalapeño pepper, minced shallot, parsley, lemon rind, and 2 cloves garlic to make a fine paste. Put it in a bowl with the shrimp, chicken, and lemon juice. Let marinate for 1 hour.

Heat the oil in a 2-quart pot. Add the sliced shallot, remaining 2 cloves garlic, chili pepper, basil, and mint. Cook for 2 minutes. Add the tomatoes, cover the pot, and turn the heat to low. Cook for 10 minutes longer. Keep warm.

Heat a broiler or grill to hot.

Wrap a strip of chicken around the outside of a shrimp. Stick a skewer through them so both are secure. Wrap the remaining chicken and shrimp in the same way, putting 3 wrapped shrimp on each of 4 skewers. Cook on the hot broiler or grill for 2 minutes a side. Slide the shrimp and chicken onto individual plates or a single platter. Serve with the wild rice and stewed tomatoes.

Serves 4

◇Carpaccio with Striped Bass and Tuna Sashimi
◇A Paillard of Turkey with Peppers and Pineapple

The raw beef and fish, representing Italy and Japan in their finest simplicity, are followed by a grilled paillard of American turkey served with Hawaiian pineapple.

You can cut all the vegetables ahead and make the fennel salad, but wait until the last minute to prepare the carpaccio and sashimi so they are impeccably fresh. Cook the turkey and its garnish while someone else clears the first course.

Carpaccio with Striped Bass and Tuna Sashimi   CAL 138

Pro 14 g, Cho 4.4 g, Fat 5.6 g, Sat 2 g, Chol 41.3 mg, Fiber 0.5 g, Ca 30.4 mg, Zn 1.8 mg, Fe 2.2 mg, Folate 17.7 mcg, Na 122.6 g, Suc 0.4 g

A Paillard of Turkey with Peppers and Pineapple   CAL 312

Pro 34.2 g, Cho 21.8 g, Fat 7.6 g, Sat 1.5 g, Chol 68.6 mg, Fiber 2.3 g, Ca 65.2 mg, Zn 2.1 mg, Fe 3 mg, Folate 62.2 mcg, Na 411.4 mg, Suc 4.4 g

Total Menu   CAL 450

Pro 48.2 g, Cho 26.2 g, Fat 13.2 g, Sat 3.5 g, Chol 109.9 mg, Fiber 2.8 g, Ca 95.6 mg, Zn 3.9 mg, Fe 5.2 mg, Folate 79.9 mcg, Na 534 mg, Suc 4.8 g

◇Carpaccio with Striped Bass and Tuna Sashimi

Carpaccio, raw beef pounded until it is paper thin, is an Italian appetizer. It pairs surprisingly well with sashimi, Japanese raw fish.

½ cup thinly sliced fennel
1 teaspoon minced jalapeño pepper
2 teaspoons olive oil
1 teaspoon red wine vinegar
2 3-ounce slices shell steak, all fat removed, about ⅛ inch thick
Freshly ground black pepper
2 ounces skinless red tuna fillet
2 ounces skinless striped bass fillet
4 1-inch pieces zucchini
2 teaspoons prepared wasabi (Japanese horseradish)
4 2-inch pieces carrot
4 teaspoons low-salt soy sauce

Mix together the fennel, jalapeño, 1 teaspoon oil, and vinegar. Set aside.

Dribble some of the remaining oil on a sheet of parchment or waxed paper. Top with a second sheet and rub together to spread the oil. Pull the papers apart. Put one slice of steak on the oiled paper. Top with the second sheet, oiled side down. Using a meat pounder or heavy pot, pound the meat in all directions until it is paper thin; it should be close to an 8-inch circle. Spoon half the fennel mixture down the center of the meat, going along the longer side. Fold over the top, then roll up. Grind black pepper on top. Trim the ends to make them even, then cut into 8 even pieces. Repeat with the remaining steak and fennel mixture.

Cut the tuna on a sharp diagonal into slices about ⅛ inch thick. Cut the striped bass at right angles to the work surface into ¼-inch-wide slices.

Cut out the center of the zucchini pieces to make small cups. Put a bit of the wasabi into each. Cut the center out of each carrot piece about an inch deep. Cut most of the wall of each carrot piece into strips to make a sort of flower. Put some soy sauce into each carrot cup.

Arrange each plate attractively. Put the carpaccio rolls together in front. Overlap the tuna slices on a separate part of the plate. Stand the bass pieces on edge in sort of steps, each piece touching the next. Put one zucchini cup and one carrot cup on each plate.

Serves 4

◇A Paillard of Turkey with Peppers and Pineapple

Sometimes it is possible to buy just a turkey breast. If you get the whole bird, use the carcass for stock and roast the legs separately. You can make the same dish with breast of chicken or pheasant.

I always use free-range turkeys. They have more taste than others. Whatever you do, avoid the frozen birds that have been injected with artificially flavored fat.

1 pound skinless turkey breast (preferably from an organic turkey)
½ ounce fresh ginger
1 tablespoon fresh lemongrass or 1 teaspoon dried lemongrass (sereh)
1 jalapeño pepper, cored and seeded
1 clove garlic
1 tablespoon olive oil
1 large scallion, thinly sliced on the diagonal
6 ounces savoy cabbage, cut into ¼-inch strips
½ large red bell pepper, cored, seeded, peeled, and cut into ¼-inch
    strips
½ large yellow bell pepper, cored, seeded, peeled, and cut into
    ¼-inch strips
½ large green bell pepper, cored, seeded, peeled, and cut into
    ¼-inch strips
¾ pound fresh rindless pineapple, cut into ¾-inch cubes
2 cups Turkey Stock (see below), reduced to ½ cup
2 tablespoons low-salt soy sauce

Working on the diagonal, cut 4 even slices (paillards) from the turkey breast. If they are more than ½ inch thick, pound them between sheets of waxed or parchment paper. Mince together the ginger, lemongrass, jalapeño pepper, and garlic. Sprinkle the seasonings over the turkey and let sit for 1 to 2 hours.

Preheat a grill or broiler until hot.

Heat the olive oil in a 10-inch nonstick skillet. Add the scallion and cook until lightly browned. Add the cabbage and cook until it begins to brown, about a minute. Don't stir too much or the vegetables will not brown. Put the bell peppers on top of the cabbage and cook another 2 minutes. Add the pineapple and stock. Sauté to mix. The total cooking time should be about 5 minutes. Keep the mixture warm while you grill the turkey.

Place the paillards on the hot grill and cook until the grate marks the meat. Rotate each 45 degrees and return to the grill, same side down, to make a diamond pattern on each piece. Turn and cook the other side. Total cooking time should be 3 to 4 minutes. Sprinkle some soy sauce on the turkey. Place each paillard in the center of an individual plate. Spoon the vegetables on top and around the turkey. Serve hot.

Serves 4

◇Turkey Stock

If you want to use the turkey legs for another dish, substitute chicken for them in the stock.

6 pounds turkey bones and drumsticks, skin removed

6 ounces onion, quartered

1 head garlic, separated but not peeled

10 ounces potato, quartered

6 ounces parsnips, halved

6 ounces celery, cut in thirds

6 ounces leek greens

3 sprigs rosemary

4 pieces mace

3 bay leaves

1 dried red chili pepper

6 cloves

4 allspice

Place the bones in a stockpot. Cover with hot water and bring to a boil. Pour out the water. Rinse off the bones. Rinse out the pot and return the bones to it with all the remaining ingredients. Add enough cold water to just cover everything.

Bring the liquid back to a boil. Remove and discard any scum and fat that rise to the surface. Lower the heat so the liquid is at a steady simmer. Partially cover and cook for 4 hours. Check the pot from time to time, removing fat and scum as necessary.

When the stock is done, pour it through a sieve lined with a dampened kitchen towel. Discard all the solids. The vegetables won't have much flavor because they have given it to the stock. Pour the stock into a clean pot and reduce by boiling, uncovered, over moderate heat until you have 1 quart (4 cups).

◇Zucchini Stuffed with Striped Bass on Tomato Sauce
◇Steamed Turkey Breast with Cabbage, Corn, and Peas

If you can, mix plates and serve the green zucchini rounds on their pool of red tomato sauce on a pale dish and the turkey breast with its cabbage, corn, and pea garnish on a black one.

Zucchini Stuffed with Striped Bass on Tomato Sauce   CAL 334

Pro 14.3 g, Cho 55.2 g, Fat 6.1 g, Sat 0.8 g, Chol 15.5 mg, Fiber 2.9 g, Ca 82.2 mg, Zn 3.2 mg, Fe 4.5 mg, Folate 85.5 mcg, Na 52.4 g, Suc 0.3 g

Steamed Turkey Breast with Cabbage, Corn, and Peas   CAL 279

Pro 37.8 g, Cho 21.8 g, Fat 5.1 g, Sat 0.7 g, Chol 90 mg, Fiber 2.3 g, Ca 86.6 mg, Zn 2.8 mg, Fe 5.4 mg, Folate 132.6 mcg, Na 75.5 mg, Suc 0.2 g

Total Menu   CAL 613

Pro 52.1 g, Cho 77 g, Fat 11.2 g, Sat 1.5 g, Chol 105.5 mg, Fiber 5.2 g, Ca 168.8 mg, Zn 6 mg, Fe 9.9 mg, Folate 218.1 mcg, Na 127.9 mg, Suc 0.5 g

◇Zucchini Stuffed with Striped Bass on Tomato Sauce

The rounds of zucchini stuffed with striped bass are enhanced by the simple tomato sauce, best made in the summer when the tomatoes are at their peak.

1 tablespoon olive oil
⅓ cup chopped shallots
1½ teaspoons minced garlic
1 pound tomatoes, peeled, cored, seeded, and chopped
1 dried red chili pepper
2 ½-pound zucchini
Freshly ground black pepper
¼ pound skinless striped bass fillet
¼ cup chopped fresh parsley
2 tablespoons chopped fresh tarragon
2 tablespoons chopped watercress leaves
1 tablespoon minced jalapeño pepper
½ pound soba (Japanese buckwheat noodles)
2 tablespoons dry white wine
6 tablespoons Chicken Stock
Pinch cayenne pepper

Heat the oil in a 1-quart pot. Add the shallots and garlic and cook until soft but not brown. Add the tomatoes and chili pepper. Cover and cook over medium heat for 30 minutes. The sauce will be thick. Remove and discard the pepper. Put the sauce in a food processor to puree. You should have about 1 cup.

Cut the ends off the zucchini and halve them lengthwise. With a spoon, scoop out and discard the seeds. Grind some black pepper on the cut edge of each piece.

Cut the fish into strips ¼ inch wide. Toss them with the parsley, tarragon, watercress, and jalapeño pepper. Fill 2 zucchini cavities with the fish, stretching the pieces along the length of the zucchini. Top with the matching piece of zucchini. Wrap each stuffed zucchini tightly in double layers of plastic wrap.

Bring water to a boil in the bottom of a steamer or wok. If your steamer bottom is a regular pot, use enough water to later cook the soba. If not, boil a separate pot of water.

Put the zucchini on the steamer and cook for 12 minutes. Set aside to rest for 5 minutes. Meanwhile, cook the soba for 4 minutes, or until done. Drain well.

Heat the wine and stock in a small pan. Bring to a boil and let cook for 1 minute. Add the tomato puree and cayenne. Cook until heated through.

Remove the zucchini from the plastic. Cut off the ends that don't have fish in them. Cut the remaining zucchini on a slight diagonal into slices about ¾ inch thick, 10 for each zucchini. Spoon some tomato sauce on each of 4 plates. Arrange 5 zucchini rounds in a partial circle on top of the sauce on each plate. Arrange the soba so it finishes the circles.

Serves 4

◇Steamed Turkey Breast with Cabbage, Corn, and Peas

This is one of the best ways to cook turkey I know. It picks up all the flavors of the marinade and stays moist from the steaming.

1 tablespoon minced jalapeño pepper

1 dried red chili pepper, minced, or 1 teaspoon flakes

1 teaspoon dried rosemary

1 cup minced fresh parsley

¼ cup minced shallots

2 cloves garlic, minced

1¼ pounds boneless turkey breast, skin still attached

½ pound green cabbage, cut into 1-inch strips

1 cup (¼ pound) corn cut from 2 medium ears or substitute frozen corn, defrosted

1 cup (5½ ounces) shelled peas

1 tablespoon white wine vinegar

1 tablespoon almond or olive oil

12 cherry tomatoes

The peppers, rosemary, parsley, shallots, and garlic should be chopped together to make a fine mixture. This can be done with a knife or in a food processor.

Loosen the skin from the turkey, but leave it attached at one end. Stuff some of the herb mixture between the skin and the turkey. Loosen the fillet from the underside of the breast. Stuff some more of the herb mixture there. You should use about two thirds of the mixture on the turkey.

Bring water to a boil in the bottom of a steamer or wok. Line a steamer basket with the cabbage. Put the turkey, skin side up, over the cabbage. Sprinkle the remaining herb mixture over the cabbage that shows. Cover the steamer and cook over the boiling water for 15 minutes. Remove the cover and sprinkle the corn over the cabbage. Cook 10 minutes longer, then add the peas over the cabbage and corn. Cook 5 minutes more.

Remove from the heat and uncover the steamer basket. Put the turkey on a plate to cool. Put the cabbage, corn, and peas in a bowl. Toss them with the vinegar and oil.

When everything has cooled to room temperature, remove the skin from the turkey and discard. Cut the turkey into thin slices. Arrange them, overlapping, on one side of a platter. Spoon the vegetables down the other side. Garnish with the cherry tomatoes.

Serves 4

NOTE: If you make the turkey for the Radish Salad with Turkey and Ham (see page 156), stuff the turkey with the herb mixture and place on a steamer rack. Sprinkle the extra herb mixture over the turkey skin. Steam over boiling water for 30 minutes.

◇Red Snapper Tartare on Cucumber
◇Radish Salad with Turkey and Ham

This is perfect for warm days when cool food is most satisfying. Serve outside with pitchers of lemony iced tea. Because everything is cold, it can, of course, be made ahead.

Red Snapper Tartare on Cucumber   CAL 133

Pro 15.8 g, Cho 6.7 g, Fat 4.2 g, Sat 0.4 g, Chol 38.6 mg, Fiber 1.1 g, Ca 64.9 mg, Zn 1.1 mg, Fe 2.1 mg, Folate 45.1 mcg, Na 62.3 g, Suc 0.1 g

Radish Salad with Turkey and Ham
CAL 260

Pro 29 g, Cho 17.3 g, Fat 9.3 g, Sat 2.3 g, Chol 70.2 mg, Fiber 1.7 g, Ca 133.5 mg, Zn 2.1 mg, Fe 4.5 mg, Folate 249.2 mcg, Na 77.8 mg, Suc 3.2 g

Total Menu   CAL 393

Pro 44.8 g, Cho 24 g, Fat 13.5 g, Sat 2.7 g, Chol 108.8 mg, Fiber 2.8 g, Ca 198.4 mg, Zn 3.2 mg, Fe 6.6 mg, Folate 294.3 mcg, Na 140.1 mg, Suc 3.3 g

◇Red Snapper Tartare on Cucumber

When I serve this on the regular menu, I use salmon as well as snapper and spread the mixture on buttered toast. The spa version is lighter and more delicate in taste. Serve it as a first course at the table or a savory before dinner.

Since the fish is not cooked, it must, of course, be very fresh. The cucumbers replace crackers so they need to have the peel on to be firm enough to hold the mixture. If your regular cucumbers are waxed, buy one of the hothouse cucumbers now on the market.

10 ounces skinless red snapper fillet
2 tablespoons minced fresh parsley
2 tablespoons minced shallots
1 tablespoon minced jalapeño pepper
2 tablespoons minced fresh chives
1 tablespoon minced cilantro (fresh coriander)
1 tablespoon brandy
Juice of ½ lemon
1 tablespoon olive oil
Freshly ground black pepper
1 large (¾-pound) cucumber with unwaxed peel
1 cup arugula leaves, washed and dried
½ red bell pepper, cored, seeded, and cut into thin strips

With a sharp knife, cut the snapper into ⅛-inch-thick slices, then strips, then ⅛-inch cubes. Do not use a food processor or the result will be mushy. Mix in the minced parsley, shallots, jalapeño pepper, chives, and cilantro along with the brandy, lemon juice, olive oil, and black pepper.

Cut the ends off the cucumber. With a fork, run the tines down the length of the cucumber all around to make even striations. Then slice it into thin rounds. Arrange them overlapping around a serving platter. Put the arugula in the center. Put the red snapper mixture on top of the arugula. Arrange the pepper strips on top as a garnish. Your guests can eat this with forks or put some fish and arugula on the cucumber rounds, using them in place of crackers.

Serves 4

◇Radish Salad
with Turkey and Ham

Radishes make a sharp base for a salad. In this case, I've added steamed turkey and ham. You could also use boiled beef, chicken, or seafood.

3 ounces red radishes, unpeeled, cut into thin rounds
¼ pound daikon (Japanese radish), peeled, cut into thin rounds
¼ pound black radish, unpeeled, shredded through the large holes of
   a 4-sided grater
Juice of ½ lemon
1 tablespoon olive oil
12 romaine lettuce leaves
2 2.5-ounce packages 2-Mamina (Japanese radish sprouts)
½ recipe Steamed Turkey Breast (see page 150), made without the
   vegetables, skin removed, and cut into julienne strips
¼ pound lean ham, cut into julienne strips
2 oranges

Put all the radishes in a bowl. Toss with the lemon juice and olive oil.

Cut the heavy cores from each lettuce leaf, leaving them V-shaped. Arrange 3 leaves around each of 4 dinner plates so the cut ends meet in the middle. Put some 2-Mamina in the center of each leaf. Spoon the radish salad in the center of each plate. Toss the turkey and ham strips together and divide among the 4 plates, on top of the radishes.

With a knife, cut the rind and all the white pith from the oranges. Then cut them into their natural sections, leaving the membranes behind. Arrange the orange sections between the lettuce leaves.

Serves 4

◇Squid Salad with Black Beans
◇Grilled Veal Steak with Tuna Sauce

The squid followed by veal with tuna sauce makes the menu Italian, but black beans are an American/Latin American influence. Prepare the squid ahead, adding the dressing at the last minute. Turn the grill on before you serve the first course and have everything ready to cook the veal, mushrooms, and sauce.

Squid Salad with Black Beans   CAL 298

Pro 24.1 g, Cho 41 g, Fat 5.4 g, Sat 0.4 g, Chol 0 mg, Fiber 3.4 g, Ca 125.3 mg, Zn 4.2 mg, Fe 5.9 mg, Folate 88.2 mcg, Na 66.2 mg, Suc 0.4 g

---

Grilled Veal Steak with Tuna Sauce CAL 389

Pro 32.1 g, Cho 15.3 g, Fat 19.5 g, Sat 5.9 g, Chol 89.8 mg, Fiber 1.3 g, Ca 82.7 mg, Zn 2.8 mg, Fe 5.4 mg, Folate 52.1 mcg, Na 119.5 mg, Suc 0 g

---

Total Menu   CAL 687

Pro 56.2 g, Cho 56.3 g, Fat 24.9 g, Sat 6.3 g, Chol 89.8 mg, Fiber 4.7 g, Ca 208 mg, Zn 7 mg, Fe 11.3 mg, Folate 140.3 mcg, Na 185.7 mg, Suc 0.4 g

---

◇Squid Salad with Black Beans

The white squid salad surrounded by a ring of black beans makes a very attractive dish with a few cherry tomatoes for color contrast.

1 cup black beans

1 quart water

4 cloves

1 2-ounce onion

2 bay leaves

1 dry red chili pepper

3 cloves garlic, 1 cracked

2 tablespoons red wine vinegar

Juice of ½ lemon

1 tablespoon olive oil

2 shallots, sliced

1 jalapeño pepper, cored, seeded, and minced

1 tablespoon chopped cilantro (fresh coriander)

10 ounces cleaned squid

12 cherry tomatoes

2 slices lime

Rinse the beans in cold water, then place them in a 2-quart pot with the quart water. Stick the cloves in the onion. Then make a slit in it and insert the bay leaves there. Add the onion to the pot with the red pepper and 2 whole cloves garlic. Bring the water to a boil, cover the pot, and let the beans simmer until they are soft and have absorbed the water, about 3 hours.

Discard the onion, red pepper, and garlic. Toss the beans with 1 tablespoon red wine vinegar.

After the beans have been cooking for about 2 hours, make the dressing. Put the cracked garlic, remaining tablespoon vinegar, lemon juice, olive oil, shallots, jalapeño pepper, and cilantro in a bowl. Whisk to mix and set aside for at least half an hour.

Bring a pot of water to a boil. Have a bowl of ice with a little water ready next to it. Hold the squid, one piece at a time, with tongs in the boiling water for 5 seconds (3 seconds, if they are small). Immediately drop them into the iced water.

When the squid is completely cool, pat it dry. Then cut it into narrow strips. You will need a very sharp knife.

When the beans are done and you are ready to serve, discard the garlic from the dressing and whisk it again. Toss the dressing with the squid. (Do not dress the squid ahead, or they will get tough.)

On each of 4 salad plates, make a ring of black beans. Put some dressed squid in the center. Garnish each plate with 3 cherry tomatoes and half a lime slice.

Serves 4

◇Grilled Veal Steak with Tuna Sauce

This variation on vitello tonnato, a famous Italian dish made with thin slices of cold veal served with a tuna mayonnaise sauce, is lighter and served hot.

4 ¼-pound pieces veal tenderloin
½ teaspoon ground rosemary
½ teaspoon freshly ground black pepper
2 tablespoons sesame oil
2 cups Veal Stock, reduced to ⅓ cup, warm
3 ounces canned tuna (drained weight) packed in water, no salt added
⅓ cup (3 ounces) unflavored low-fat yogurt
2 tablespoons minced jalapeño pepper
½ ounce fresh ginger, cut into fine shreds (4 teaspoons)
2 ounces shallots, thinly sliced
½ clove garlic, minced
1 tablespoon (½ ounce) pine nuts (pignoli)
6 ounces wild mushrooms, roughly chopped
1 pound zucchini, cut into julienne strips or thin rounds

Preheat a grill or broiler until hot.

The veal pieces need to be pounded to make equal steaks about ¾ inch thick. Place them one at a time on a clean, damp towel. Fold the towel over to cover the meat and pinch the sides together firmly but gently. Using a meat pounder or heavy pot, pound the meat until it is the proper thickness. As the meat spreads out, loosen your grip on the towel. When all the meat is ready, mix together the rosemary and pepper and spread it all over the meat. (The easiest way to make a powdery mixture is to put equal parts of rosemary and pepper in a spice grinder and grind until fine. Use 1 teaspoon of the mixture.) Rub 2 teaspoons sesame oil on the meat.

Put the reduced stock, drained tuna, yogurt, and half the jalapeño pepper in a food processor. Process until smooth. Put the sauce mixture into a small pan ready to heat just before serving.

When the grill is hot, place the veal on it at an angle. Cook until nicely seared. Rotate each piece 45 degrees and put it back on the grill with the same side down until seared. Each piece should have a clear diamond pattern on it. Turn and cook in the same way on the other side. The total cooking time should be about 7 minutes. Remove to one side of a warm platter. Sprinkle the ginger shreds on top. Keep warm.

While the veal is cooking, heat the remaining 4 teaspoons sesame oil in a skillet. Add the shallots, garlic, and remaining tablespoon jalapeño pepper. Cook until lightly browned. Add the pine nuts and let brown. Add the mushrooms and zucchini and cook until the mushrooms wilt. Arrange the mushrooms and zucchini on the other side of the platter with the veal. Keep warm.

Quickly heat the tuna sauce. Put it in a sauce boat and serve with the veal and vegetables.

Serves 4

◇Sautéed Wild Asparagus with King Crabmeat
◇Roast Veal Tenderloin with Ginger and Sage

This meal is sure to impress your guests and make them feel pampered. After the luxurious asparagus with crabmeat, there are slices of veal tenderloin with spaetzle, a childhood favorite of mine. The first course takes only a few minutes to cook. The night before, marinate the veal and blanch the snow peas and sage leaves to reheat the next day. You may also reduce the stock.

The spaetzle is the most time-consuming part of the meal. If you are well organized, cook it while the veal is cooking. If you prefer, make it before you start the veal and reheat briefly in vegetable stock just before serving.

Sautéed Wild Asparagus with King Crabmeat CAL 170

Pro 15.7 g, Cho 13.3 g, Fat 7.3 g, Sat 2.8 g, Chol 37.5 mg, Fiber 2.4 g, Ca 64.1 mg, Zn 2 mg, Fe 2.2 mg, Folate 91.4 mcg, Na 118.7 mg, Suc 0 g

Roast Veal Tenderloin with Ginger and Sage CAL 486

Pro 31.3 g, Cho 41.3 g, Fat 18 g, Sat 5.7 g, Chol 74.7 mg, Fiber 2.6 g, Ca 114.2 mg, Zn 3.2 mg, Fe 5.6 mg, Folate 90.3 mcg, Na 121.8 mg, Suc 1.2 g

Total Menu CAL 656

Pro 47 g, Cho 54.6 g, Fat 25.3 g, Sat 8.5 g, Chol 112.2 mg, Fiber 5 g, Ca 178.3 mg, Zn 5.2 mg, Fe 7.8 mg, Folate 181.7 mcg, Na 240.5 mg, Suc 1.2 g

◇Sautéed Wild Asparagus with King Crabmeat

Wild asparagus are pencil thin. If they are not available, get the thinnest asparagus in the market for this recipe. The woody ends, too fibrous for pleasant eating, can be cooked for soup.

I try to use king crabmeat for this dish because the red in the meat is more attractive than all-white lump crabmeat.

1 pound wild asparagus
1 large (6-ounce) red bell pepper
1 large (6-ounce) yellow bell pepper
1 tablespoon corn oil
2 tablespoons (1 ounce) pine nuts (pignoli)
¼ cup thinly sliced shallots
1 tablespoon minced jalapeño pepper
½ pound king crabmeat, in strips
2 teaspoons low-salt soy sauce

Bring a pot of water to a boil. Cut the asparagus tips off on the diagonal. Cut off and discard the fibrous bottom of each stalk. Cut the remaining stalks on a sharp diagonal into pieces about 2 inches long and ½ inch wide. Drop in the boiling water and cook for 1 minute. Drain well.

Peel and core the peppers, then divide them into their natural sections and remove the seeds and ribs. Cut each section crosswise into ⅛-inch strips.

In a nonstick pan, heat the oil. Add the pine nuts and let them brown slightly, about 1 minute. Add the shallots and jalapeño pepper and cook a minute to brown. Stir in the asparagus to heat, followed by the pepper strips and crabmeat. When everything is hot, add the soy sauce.

Serves 4

◇Roast Veal Tenderloin with Ginger and Sage

The veal tenderloin is a flavorful cut providing it is not overcooked and allowed to dry out. I often cook meat this way, browning it on top of the stove and then putting it in the oven to finish cooking.

½ teaspoon red pepper flakes
1 tablespoon minced fresh ginger
½ teaspoon chopped fresh sage leaves plus 20 whole leaves, stems cut off
1 tablespoon minced garlic
1 pound veal tenderloin, cut into 4 even pieces
1 tablespoon olive oil
1 pound snow peas
½ cup dry white wine
1 teaspoon arrowroot
2 cups Veal Stock, reduced to 1 cup
1 tablespoon corn oil
2 shallots, minced
Juice of ½ lemon
1 recipe Whole-Wheat Spaetzle (see below)

Mix together the red pepper flakes, ginger, chopped sage leaves, and garlic. Rub mixture on the veal pieces with the olive oil. Place in a pan, cover with plastic wrap, and leave for 2 hours at room temperature or refrigerate overnight.

Preheat the oven to 400° F.

Place an 8- to 10-inch ovenproof skillet over a burner until hot. Add the veal in a single layer and cook until browned on all sides, about 2 minutes. Place the pan in the preheated oven to roast for 5 minutes. Turn each piece over, return to the oven, and roast 5 minutes longer. Turn the oven off. Place the veal on a heated platter, cover it loosely with foil, and keep it warm in the turned-off oven.

While the veal cooks (or the night before), bring a pot of water to a boil. Dip the whole sage leaves in for about 2 seconds to blanch. Drain and set aside for the garnish. Put the snow peas in the same water and blanch for about 1 minute. Cool. Drain well and set aside.

Mix 1 teaspoon wine with the arrowroot. Set aside.

Add the stock and remaining wine to the skillet the veal cooked in and scrape the bottom with a wooden spoon to deglaze. Bring this sauce to a boil and cook for about 90 seconds. Stir the arrowroot mixture and add it to the skillet along with any juices the veal gives off as it sits. You should have about ¾ cup sauce—if there is too much, cook a little longer; if too thick, add some water. Keep the sauce warm.

Heat the corn oil in a clean skillet. Add the shallots and cook until lightly browned. Add the lemon juice (just squeeze it directly into the pan) and stir to deglaze. On medium heat, add the snow peas and cook, tossing often, just until heated through.

Have ready 4 heated dinner plates. Cut one piece of veal into 6 rounds, each about ½ inch thick. Arrange them, slightly overlapping, on one side of the plate. Place a sage leaf between each pair of rounds. Place a quarter of the snow peas in the middle of the plate and a quarter of the spaetzle on the other side. Repeat with the remaining plates. Spoon some of the sauce over the veal, serving the rest in a sauceboat.

Serves 4

◇Whole-Wheat Spaetzle

Spaetzle are small, thin dumplings made by flicking strips of dough off a plate or board into boiling water. They are often confused with knoepfli, small buttons, made with machines that resemble food mills. Housewives in my native Switzerland have traditionally been judged on the quality of their spaetzle.

I adapted the recipe for Spa Cuisine by using egg whites and whole-wheat flour instead of whole eggs and white flour. When possible, cook them in vegetable stock rather than water.

1 small (1-ounce) leek, cleaned and minced
1 jalapeño pepper, cored, seeded, and minced
2 egg whites
Pinch freshly grated nutmeg
⅓ cup water
1 cup (5 ounces) whole-wheat flour, sifted
Vegetable Stock or water

Put the leek, pepper, egg whites, and nutmeg in a mixing bowl with the water. Whisk briefly to mix. Add the flour and stir until evenly combined. The dough should come together as a thick, sticky batter.

Bring the stock or water to a boil in a 10-inch skillet. Lower the heat so the water gently simmers. Watch the water and raise or lower the heat as necessary during cooking to keep the water at a constant temperature. Place the batter on a flat board or plate. With a wet spatula or knife, cut off thin strips of dough about 2½ inches long and drop them in the simmering water. Dip your spatula frequently into the water to keep it wet. When all the dough has been used, cook for 2 minutes. Drain and serve hot.

Serves 4

◇Clam Chowder
◇Escalope of Veal
with Mustard Seeds

The chunky clam chowder makes an excellent introduction to the spicier veal coated in mustard seeds. As with most soups, the chowder can be made ahead and reheated. You can prepare it when you cook the beans, which can be reheated just before you quickly cook the veal.

Clam Chowder   CAL 168

*Pro 12.4 g, Cho 11.8 g, Fat 5.4 g, Sat 0.4 g, Chol 35.6 mg, Fiber 1.8 g,
Ca 64.9 mg, Zn 1.3 mg, Fe 4.1 mg, Folate 45 mcg, Na 133.5 mg,
Suc 0 g*

Escalope of Veal with Mustard Seeds
CAL 369

*Pro 26.5 g, Cho 26.7 g, Fat 18.7 g, Sat 5.7 g, Chol 75.1 mg, Fiber 5.7 g,
Ca 197.5 mg, Zn 4.3 mg, Fe 5.3 mg, Folate 118.8 mcg, Na 73.4 mg,
Suc 0 g*

Total Menu   CAL 537

*Pro 38.9 g, Cho 38.5 g, Fat 24.1 g, Sat 6.1 g, Chol 110.7 mg, Fiber 7.5 g,
Ca 262.4 mg, Zn 5.6 mg, Fe 9.4 mg, Folate 163.8 mcg, Na 206.9 mg,
Suc 0 g*

◇Clam Chowder

This is more like cioppino, an Italian-American fish soup, than either Manhattan or New England clam chowder.

16 cherrystone clams, washed well
¼ cup water
1 tablespoon olive oil
2 large shallots, sliced
2 jalapeño peppers, cored, seeded, and minced
1 clove garlic, minced
1 2-ounce piece of fennel or peeled parsnip, cut into ¼-inch cubes
   (½ cup)
1 large (2-ounce) stalk celery, cut into ¼-inch slices
1 3-ounce tomato, peeled, seeded, and roughly chopped
1 green bell pepper, cored, seeded, and cut into ¼-inch squares
1 yellow bell pepper, cored, seeded, and cut into ¼-inch squares
1 dried fennel branch, if using parsnip
2 cups Fish Stock or water
1 teaspoon saffron threads
4 teaspoons snipped fresh chives

Put the clams in a pot with the water. Cover and cook over medium-high heat for about 10 minutes, or until the clam shells open. Remove from the heat. Pull out the clams, reserving the liquid, discarding the shells. Chop the clams into ¼-inch pieces. Strain and measure the liquid. You should have 1 cup. If not, add water.

Heat the oil in a 3-quart pot. Add the shallots, jalapeño peppers, garlic, fennel, and celery. Cook until lightly browned. Add the reserved clam liquid along with the chopped clams, tomato, bell peppers, the fennel branch if you are using it, and fish stock. Simmer for 40 minutes. Stir in the saffron and cook a minute longer to dissolve the threads and give the soup a rich, golden color.

Top each bowl with 1 teaspoon snipped chives.

Serves 4

◇Escalope of Veal with Mustard Seeds

Sometimes the simplest preparations are the best.

4 teaspoons black mustard seeds
1¼ pounds veal tenderloin, cut into 8 slices
1 tablespoon corn oil
Freshly ground black pepper
1 recipe Braised Broad Beans (see below)

Press some mustard seeds on each piece of veal.

Heat the oil in a 10-inch nonstick pan. Add the veal in a single layer and cook for 45 seconds. Turn and cook for a minute more. Grind some black pepper on each piece.

Serve with the broad beans.

Serves 4

◇Braised Broad Beans

In my family, broad beans were always cooked with plenty of bacon fat. I was delighted to find how good these are with the turnip sauce.

1 tablespoon olive oil

1 cup sliced shallots

4 cloves garlic, sliced

2 jalapeño peppers, cored, seeded, and minced

¾ pound (4 medium) turnips, peeled, halved, and cut into 1-inch slices

2 pounds broad beans, ends broken off, halved

2 cups Vegetable Stock

Heat the oil in a 2-quart saucepan. Add the shallots, garlic, and jalapeño peppers. Cook until lightly browned. Add the turnips, beans, and stock. Cook, covered, over medium heat for about 45 minutes. The beans should be soft, the turnips, overcooked. Remove the pan from the heat. Put the solids in a bowl, leaving the liquid in the pan. Pick out the turnips and push them through a strainer into the liquid still in the pot. Bring to a boil. Add the beans and cook just to reheat.

Serves 4

◇Stuffed Kohlrabi
◇Cold Roast Loin of Veal with Salsify

From the delicate kohlrabies stuffed with vegetables to the spicy veal with yams and salsify in a chunky vinaigrette, this unusual menu is sure to delight friends.

The veal needs to be cooked ahead to give it time to cool. The kohlrabies can be stuffed ahead, but are best if baked just before serving. The salsify is fine hot, warm, or at room temperature.

Stuffed Kohlrabi   CAL 144

Pro 8.3 g, Cho 19.4 g, Fat 5.4 g, Sat 0.5 g, Chol 0 mg, Fiber 3 g, Ca 142.5 mg, Zn 0.5 mg, Fe 3 mg, Folate 84.5 mcg, Na 39.5 mg, Suc 0.4 g

Cold Roast Loin of Veal with Salsify

CAL 510

Pro 28.7 g, Cho 55.7 g, Fat 19.4 g, Sat 6.2 g, Chol 81.7 mg, Fiber 4.5 g, Ca 108.7 mg, Zn 3.6 mg, Fe 6.5 mg, Folate 85.6 mcg, Na 129.2 mg, Suc 1.2 g

Total Menu   CAL 654

Pro 37 g, Cho 75.1 g, Fat 24.8 g, Sat 6.7 g, Chol 81.7 mg, Fiber 7.5 g, Ca 251.2 mg, Zn 4.1 mg, Fe 9.5 mg, Folate 170.1 mcg, Na 168.7 mg, Suc 1.6 g

◇Stuffed Kohlrabi

Kohlrabies, not commonly used here, are native to Europe. The name means "cabbage turnip" in German. Generally round in shape, this pale green vegetable has leaves that are usually removed, although they are perfectly edible. Fresh kohlrabies should be firm with a thin rind.

1 dried red chili pepper
4 8-ounce kohlrabies
1 tablespoon olive oil
1 clove garlic, minced
2 teaspoons minced jalapeño pepper
½ cup chopped onion
½ cup chopped fresh fennel
½ cup chopped red bell pepper
½ cup chopped fresh parsley
⅛ teaspoon caraway seeds
6 fresh sage leaves, minced, or 1 teaspoon dried sage
¼ pound tofu, cut into ¼-inch cubes
¼ cup Chicken Stock or other stock

Bring a pot of water with the dried red pepper to a boil.

Peel each kohlrabi and cut off the top ½ inch. Using a melon baller, scoop out the inside until you have a shell about ½ inch wide. Save all the kohlrabi you scoop out and roughly chop it. Drop the shells into the boiling water and cook until just done, about 15 minutes. Drain and pat dry.

Preheat the oven to 350° F.

Heat the oil in a skillet. Add the garlic and jalapeño pepper. Cook a minute, then add the onion and fennel. Cook until lightly brown. Remove the mixture to a bowl. Add the red bell pepper, parsley, caraway, sage, kohlrabi pieces, and tofu. Divide the mixture into 4 parts and use it to stuff each kohlrabi.

Place the kohlrabi in a baking dish, add ¼ cup stock to the bottom of the dish, and bake in the preheated oven until done, about 30 minutes.

Serves 4

◇Cold Roast Loin of Veal with Salsify

Salsify, a vegetable few Americans know, looks like thick black twigs in its raw state. Also called oyster plant, it has a delicate flavor enhanced here by the vinaigrette. I urge you to look for it and try this recipe.

5 dried red chili peppers
Rind and juice of ½ lime
2 bay leaves
1½ teaspoons mace
1-pound piece loin of veal
2 tablespoons olive oil
1 cup milk
2 lemons
1 pound salsify
¼ cup dry white wine
2 tablespoons white wine vinegar
2 cloves garlic, peeled
1 2-inch piece orange rind
⅓ cup minced onion
¾ cup peeled, seeded, and diced tomato
¾ cup diced green bell pepper
Freshly ground black pepper
2 ½-pound yams

Put 2 chili peppers, lime rind, bay leaves, and mace in a spice or coffee grinder. Run until the mixture is very fine. Sprinkle the lime juice over the veal. Coat with the chili pepper mixture. Set aside to marinate for 2 to 3 hours.

Preheat the oven to 400° F.

Heat 1 tablespoon oil in an 8-inch ovenproof skillet. Add the veal and cook for 1 minute. Turn the meat over with tongs and place it in the preheated oven. Cook another 16 minutes or until just pink in the center. Remove from the oven. Set aside and let cool to room temperature.

Put the milk and 1 quart water in a 10-inch skillet. Halve the lemons and squeeze them into the liquid. Drop in the rinds. The milk and lemon juice will keep the salsify from getting dark once it is peeled. Trim the roots off the salsify and peel the pieces. Cut them into 2-inch sections and drop into the prepared liquid with 2 chili peppers. Bring the liquid to a boil, lower the heat, and simmer until the salsify is cooked through, 20 to 30 minutes.

While the salsify is cooking, make the vinaigrette. Heat the wine, vinegar, garlic, remaining chili pepper, remaining olive oil, and orange rind in a saucepan. Simmer for 10 minutes. Remove and discard the garlic, red pepper, and orange rind. Add the onion and simmer for 2 to 3 minutes. Add the tomato and bell pepper and simmer another 3 minutes. Grind in some black pepper.

When the salsify is done, strain it, discarding the chili peppers and lemons. Toss the hot salsify with the hot vinaigrette.

Bring a pot of water to a boil. Add the yams and cook until soft. Peel each yam and cut each into 6 slices. Arrange them on one side of a platter. Cut the veal into thin slices and arrange those on the other side. Serve the salsify in a bowl on the side.

Serves 4

◇Italian Minestrone
◇Sole and Veal
on Pecan Rice

This dinner starts with a chunky minestrone full of vegetables, beans, and macaroni, followed by an unusual rice dish that combines veal and sole with fruits. The soup and rice can be done ahead, the veal and sole at the end.

Italian Minestrone   CAL 269

Pro 10.7 g, Cho 34.4 g, Fat 4.6 g, Sat 0.3 g, Chol 0 mg, Fiber 2.6 g, Ca 79.6 mg, Zn 1.4 mg, Fe 4.7 mg, Folate 69.5 mcg, Na 127.4 mg, Suc 0.9 g

Sole and Veal on Pecan Rice   CAL 429

Pro 24.7 g, Cho 36.4 g, Fat 19.8 g, Sat 4.4 g, Chol 70.2 mg, Fiber 1.3 g, Ca 37.9 mg, Zn 3.1 mg, Fe 3.2 mg, Folate 25.7 mcg, Na 141.1 mg, Suc 5.2 g

Total Menu   CAL 698

Pro 35.4 g, Cho 70.8 g, Fat 24.4 g, Sat 4.7 g, Chol 70.2 mg, Fiber 3.9 g, Ca 117.5 mg, Zn 4.5 mg, Fe 7.9 mg, Folate 95.2 mcg, Na 268.5 mg, Suc 6.1 g

◇Italian Minestrone

The Italians serve minestrone either hot or at room temperature. This soup is fine either way. If you decide to serve it cool, spoon it into individual bowls and refrigerate. Take it out an hour before serving to warm up a bit. Sprinkle each serving with ½ teaspoon hot safflower oil.

1 tablespoon safflower oil
½ cup (2 ounces) diced onion
2 cloves garlic, minced
1 tablespoon minced jalapeño pepper
½ cup (2 ounces) diced celery
½ cup (1½ ounces) leek, cut into 1-inch pieces
½ cup (2 ounces) diced zucchini
1 cup (¼ pound) diced carrots
½ cup (2 ounces) diced potato
One 3-ounce tomato, peeled, seeded, and diced (½ cup)
1 cup (¼ pound) broad beans, cut into 1-inch pieces
½ cup (2 ounces) diced parsnip
½ cup white beans, soaked in cold water overnight
1 quart Beef or Chicken Stock
¼ cup (1 ounce) whole-wheat macaroni or tubetti
¼ cup fresh Italian parsley leaves

Heat the oil in a 3-quart pot. Add the onion, garlic, jalapeño pepper, celery, and leek. Cook for 3 to 4 minutes, until soft but not brown. Add the zucchini, carrots, potato, tomato, broad beans, parsnip, and drained white beans along with the stock. Bring to a boil, lower the heat, and cook, partially covered, for 1 hour.

Add the pasta and cook 15 minutes longer. Stir in the parsley and cook 5 minutes more. Serve either hot or cool (see introduction).

Serves 4

◇Sole and Veal on Pecan Rice

At the Grand Hotel, in Stockholm, riz pilaf is made with pork and beef. I like this lighter version with its Polynesian overtones.

1 tablespoon corn oil
½ pound veal tenderloin, cut into julienne strips
½ pound skinless sole fillet, cut into julienne strips
¼ pound pineapple, cut into ½-inch chunks
1 red bell pepper, cored, seeded, peeled, and cut into ⅛-inch strips
1 6-ounce banana, peeled, halved lengthwise, then cut into ½-inch slices
½ teaspoon curry powder
Juice of ½ lemon
1 recipe Pecan Rice (see page 42)
Freshly ground black pepper

Heat the oil in a 10-inch skillet. Add the veal and sole. Cook, tossing, for 1 minute. Add the pineapple, pepper, and banana along with the curry and lemon juice. Cook for another 4 to 5 minutes, or until everything is hot.

Put the rice in a ring on a platter. Spoon the sole and veal mixture into the center. Grind black pepper on top.

Serves 4

◇Romaine, Endive, Beet, and Grapefruit Salad
◇Matembré, Stuffed Flank Steak

This salad is superb winter fare that hints of warmer days to come. The matembré makes an elegant but substantial main dish. Prepare the ingredients and dressing for the salad ahead, but wait until the last minute to assemble the plates so everything is fresh. Cook the beef ahead, slice it and reheat with the freshly made sauce before serving.

Romaine, Endive, Beet, and Grapefruit Salad   CAL 219

Pro 3.9 g, Cho 29.1 g, Fat 11.7 g, Sat 0.9 g, Chol 0 mg, Fiber 1.6 g, Ca 106.3 mg, Zn 1.6 mg, Fe 2.6 mg, Folate 200 mcg, Na 31.7 mg, Suc 5.1 g

---

Matembré, Stuffed Flank Steak   CAL 272

Pro 29.8 g, Cho 14.8 g, Fat 7.4 g, Sat 3.3 g, Chol 87.1 mg, Fiber 1.4 g, Ca 41.5 mg, Zn 4 mg, Fe 5.3 mg, Folate 44.7 mcg, Na 203.9 mg, Suc 1 g

---

Total Menu   CAL 491

Pro 33.7 g, Cho 43.9 g, Fat 19.1 g, Sat 4.2 g, Chol 87.1 mg, Fiber 3 g, Ca 147.8 mg, Zn 5.6 mg, Fe 7.9 mg, Folate 244.7 mcg, Na 235.6 mg, Suc 6.1 g

---

◇Romaine, Endive, Beet, and Grapefruit Salad

Not only is this salad with its variety of shapes and colors so beautiful to look at, the mixture of flavors and textures are extraordinary.

1 ½-pound head romaine lettuce
1 ¼-pound endive
1 1½-pound ruby red grapefruit or 2 smaller grapefruits
1 6-ounce beet
2 tablespoons red wine vinegar
1 teaspoon balsamic vinegar
2 tablespoons safflower oil
1 teaspoon honey
1 jalapeño pepper, cored, seeded, and minced
½ cup minced shallots
1 ounce (about ¼ cup) chopped walnuts

Cut the ribs out of the large romaine leaves and discard. Separate the endive into leaves, discarding the root.

With a knife, cut the rind and all the white pith from the grapfruit, then cut it into its natural sections, leaving the membrane behind. Set aside.

Bring a small pot of water to a boil. Add the beet and cook until a skewer can just barely get through. Remove and cool slightly. Slip the skin off with your fingers. Cut the beet into julienne strips about ⅛ inch wide.

In a mixing bowl, beat the wine and balsamic vinegars with the oil, honey, jalapeño pepper, and shallots. Add the romaine and endive leaves and toss to coat.

Arrange some of the romaine toward the top of each of 4 salad plates. Put the grapefruit sections across the bottom of the lettuce. Put the endive leaves below the grapefruit, pointing up, so the tips partially cover the grapefruit. Place the beet strips across the bottom of the endive. Scatter the walnuts on top. Spoon any remaining dressing over each plate.

Serves 4

◇Matembré, Stuffed Flank Steak

In South America, matembré is a common dish. Butterflied flank steak is spread with vegetables, then rolled up and braised. When sliced, each pinwheel round with its firm vegetables is like a mosaic. The filling almost always includes hard-boiled eggs and bread crumbs, ingredients I left out to make a lighter dish. Try to cut the vegetables into neat cubes to make a prettier roll.

½ cup (2 ounces) diced carrots
½ cup (2 ounces) diced celery
½ cup (2 ounces) diced red onion
½ cup (2 ounces) diced red bell pepper
½ cup (2 ounces) diced green bell pepper
½ cup (2½ ounces) peas
2 cloves garlic, minced
1 tablespoon minced jalapeño pepper
2 slices whole-wheat bread, soaked in water until soft, squeezed dry
1 1¼-pound flank steak
1 cup Beef Stock
1 teaspoon arrowroot dissolved in 1 tablespoon water

Preheat the oven to 375° F.

Bring a large pot of water to a boil. Add the carrots, celery, onion, bell peppers, and peas. Cook for 1 minute. Drain well. Set aside in a bowl and mix with the garlic, jalapeño pepper, and bread.

Butterfly the flank steak by cutting along the long side with your knife parallel to the work surface. Divide the beef evenly in 2, cutting until about ½ inch is still attached. Open the beef up like a book. If it is more than ½ inch thick, pound it with a meat pounder or heavy pot until even.

Spread all but about 1 cup vegetables over the meat, then carefully roll it up, beginning at one short end, into a tight jelly roll. Using kitchen string, neatly tie the roll at 1-inch intervals. Also tie around the edges. Add any vegetables that fall out to those you reserved. Place the roll into a 9-x-5-inch baking dish.

Roast the roll in the preheated oven for 1 hour, giving it a quarter turn every 10 minutes in the beginning so it will brown evenly. Remove to a carving board and let rest for 20 minutes—it is very difficult to get even slices when the meat is hot. Cut the strings and carefully pull them away from the meat so it does not tear. Cut the beef neatly into ½-inch slices. Place them, overlapping, in a baking/serving dish. (You may cook the meat early in the day, or even the day before, but do not slice it until you are ready to reheat and serve.)

Heat the stock with the reserved vegetables. When the liquid is boiling, stir in the dissolved arrowroot. Cook just until the sauce starts to thicken. Spoon it over the meat and return it to the oven for 10 minutes to reheat.

Serves 4

◇Whole-Wheat Fettuccine with Lobster
◇Skillet Steak with Bell Peppers

This dinner will convince those who think eating nutritiously means having to give up foods like steak and pasta that they are mistaken. The potatoes and bell peppers cook the longest, but you needn't stand over them. The rest of the meal is fairly quick.

o

Whole-Wheat Fettuccine with Lobster
CAL 261

Pro 12.9 g, Cho 36 g, Fat 6.4 g, Sat 1.6 g, Chol 41.9 g, Fiber 0.7 g, Ca 101.7 mg, Zn 2.3 mg, Fe 2.8 mg, Folate 42 mcg, Na 121.4 mg, Suc 0.1 g

Skillet Steak with Bell Peppers   CAL 378

Pro 29.6 g, Cho 37.3 g, Fat 13.1 g, Sat 3.6 g, Chol 67.6 mg, Fiber 2.9 g, Ca 44.4 mg, Zn 3.7 mg, Fe 5 mg, Folate 54.2 mcg, Na 448.6 mg, Suc 1 g

Total Menu   CAL 639

Pro 42.5 g, Cho 73.3 g, Fat 19.5 g, Sat 5.2 g, Chol 109.5 mg, Fiber 3.6 g, Ca 146.1 mg, Zn 6 mg, Fe 7.8 mg, Folate 96.2 mcg, Na 570 mg, Suc 1.1 g

◇Whole-Wheat Fettuccine with Lobster

Pasta dishes can be extraordinary or mundane. This one, made with chunks of lobster, falls into the first category, but is surprisingly easy to make. Use the meat from both the tail and the claws. Claw meat, being redder, is particularly pretty.

6 ounces savoy cabbage, yellow and green leaves, cut into ¼-inch strips
½ pound fresh whole-wheat fettuccine
1 tablespoon corn oil
1 clove garlic, minced
¼ cup sliced shallots
2 scallions, cut diagonally into thin slices
1 tablespoon chopped fresh tarragon, or 1 teaspoon dried tarragon
6 ounces cooked lobster, cut into ½-inch cubes (see note)
½ cup Fish Stock or reserved pasta liquid
¼ cup low-fat sour cream
Freshly ground black pepper

Bring a large pot of water to a boil. Add the cabbage and cook until soft, about 1 minute. Drain, reserving the liquid. Rinse under cold water, squeeze dry, and set aside.

Bring the water back to a boil. Add the fettuccine and cook until barely done, about 4 minutes. Drain and rinse under cold water. Reserve ½ cup liquid if you are using that in place of fish stock.

Heat the oil in an 8- to 10-inch nonstick skillet. Add the garlic and shallots and cook until lightly browned, about 1 minute. Add the scallions, cabbage, and tarragon. Cook for 1 minute. Then add the lobster and fettuccine with the fish stock or pasta liquid. Toss and cook for about a minute to heat through. Add the sour cream and stir to roughly mix. A few white streaks should show. Season with black pepper to taste.

Serves 4

NOTE: To get 6 ounces cooked lobster meat, you will need a 1½-pound lobster. Cook it ahead, dropping it in boiling water for 7 to 8 minutes.

◇Skillet Steak with Bell Peppers

Peppers are, as is obvious to anyone flipping through these recipes, among my favorite foods. Here they embellish a simply cooked steak. The crisp potato skins are so good it shows how unnecessary all the complex toppings are.

2 11-ounce baking potatoes
2 tablespoons corn oil
1 5-ounce onion, cut into 1-inch chunks
2 cloves garlic, minced
1 large jalapeño pepper, cored, seeded, and thinly sliced
1 6-ounce yellow bell pepper, cored, seeded, and cut into 1½-inch squares
1 6-ounce green bell pepper, cored, seeded, and cut into 1½-inch squares
1 6-ounce red bell pepper, cored, seeded, and cut into 1½-inch squares
Freshly ground black pepper
4 ¼-pound sirloin strip steaks, trimmed of all fat

Preheat the oven to 400° F. Put the potatoes on a rack in the oven and bake until they are soft through, about 1 hour. Cut each potato in half lengthwise and carefully scoop out most of the insides. (Reserve the insides for another meal, to thicken soup, or to make into potato salad —none of which is part of Spa Cuisine.) Return the shells to the oven and bake another half hour, or until brown and crisp.

Heat 1 tablespoon oil in a 10-inch nonstick pan. Add the onion, garlic, and jalapeño pepper. Cook until lightly browned, about 3 minutes. Add the bell peppers and simmer slowly until soft, 15 to 20 minutes.

Just before you are ready to serve, heat the remaining tablespoon oil in a 10-inch cast-iron skillet. Grind pepper on the steaks and cook them over high heat until done, 3 minutes a side for medium rare.

Serve each person one steak with some of the pepper mixture and a potato shell.

Serves 4

◇Oriental Soup
◇Steak au Poivre

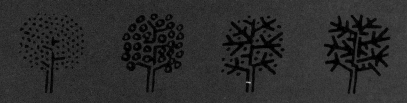

Another mixing of East and West, this delicate soup is followed by a hearty peppered steak. If you set up the soup ahead, it will be finished in a matter of minutes. Start cooking the turnips before you have the soup but wait to do the steaks until just before serving.

Oriental Soup   CAL 149

Pro 9.9 g, Cho 25.7 g, Fat 1.5 g, Sat 0.3 g, Chol 29.3 mg, Fiber 1.7 g, Ca 37.1 mg, Zn 1.3 mg, Fe 1.1 mg, Folate 53 mcg, Na 88.1 mg, Suc 0 g

Steak au Poivre   CAL 504

Pro 33.9 g, Cho 36.5 g, Fat 16.9 g, Sat 4.8 g, Chol 73.6 mg, Fiber 2 g, Ca 95.8 mg, Zn 4.9 mg, Fe 7.1 mg, Folate 42.6 mcg, Na 213.7 mg, Suc 1.8 g

Total Menu   CAL 653

Pro 43.8 g, Cho 62.2 g, Fat 18.4 g, Sat 5.1 g, Chol 102.9 mg, Fiber 3.7 g, Ca 132.9 mg, Zn 6.2 mg, Fe 8.2 mg, Folate 95.6 mcg, Na 301.8 mg, Suc 1.8 g

◇Oriental Soup

This soup is made with Japanese stock called dashi. Much quicker to make than Western stocks, it uses seaweed and dry fish flakes. The ingredients are available at all Japanese shops as well as stores carrying general oriental foods. If you prefer, substitute 6 cups fish stock.

1 10- to 12-inch piece kombu (Japanese kelp)

6 cups cold water

2 5-gram packages bonito flakes

1/4-pound carrot (preferably a part of a thick carrot)

2 ounces fresh shiitake mushrooms, or 4 dried shiitake soaked in cold water for 1 hour

2 ounces cellophane bean thread noodles, broken into 2-inch pieces

1 100-gram (3.5-ounce) package enoki mushrooms

1 2.5-ounce package 2-Mamina (Japanese radish sprouts)

2 dried red chili peppers

1 teaspoon finely julienned ginger

1/4 pound daikon (Japanese radish), cut into julienne strips

2 ounces water chestnuts, cut into thin rounds

2 ounces boneless, skinless chicken breast, cut into julienne strips

3 ounces shelled, deveined shrimp, cut into julienne strips

2 scallions, cut diagonally into 1-inch pieces

1 teaspoon low-salt soy sauce

Freshly ground black pepper

Place the kombu in a pot with the cold water. Bring to a boil. Remove and discard the kombu. Add the bonito flakes and remove the pot from the heat. Let it sit until the fish flakes settle on the bottom. Pour the stock through a strainer lined with a damp kitchen towel. Discard the solids.

Using a knife or a metal flower-shaped cutter, trim the carrot piece so it looks like petals, then cut into thin rounds.

If using dried shiitake, drain and squeeze dry. Whether fresh or dried, cut away the stems (they are too tough to eat). Slice the caps into ¼-inch strips.

Place the cellophane noodles in a bowl. Add boiling water to cover. Let them sit for 5 minutes, or until completely soft. Drain well.

Have ready a heated 2-quart soup tureen. Put the cellophane noodles, shiitake and enoki mushrooms in the bowl along with the 2-Mamina.

Bring the stock back to a boil with the chili peppers and ginger. Add the carrots, daikon, water chestnuts, and chicken. Stir to mix well. When the stock starts boiling again, add the shrimp and scallions. When it returns to the boil, ladle into the hot tureen. Season with the soy sauce and black pepper.

Serves 4

◇Steak au Poivre

When choosing steaks, ask for choice, not prime, which have more fat.

¼ cup water
1 tablespoon honey
1 pound turnips, peeled and cut into 1-inch chunks
1 dried red chili pepper
4 teaspoons crushed peppercorns (black, white, green, red, or a mixture)
1 tablespoon olive oil
4 ¼-pound sirloin steaks, all fat removed, or filet mignon
½ cup dry red wine
2 cups Beef or Veal Stock
¼ cup low-fat sour cream
1 recipe Wild Rice (see page 90)

Put the water and honey in the bottom of a 2-quart saucepan. Add the turnips and red pepper. Do not mix. Bring the liquid to a boil, cover the pan, and cook slowly for 20 minutes, or until the turnips are soft. Toss to coat them with the honey. Discard the red pepper.

Press 1 teaspoon crushed pepper onto each steak, dividing it between the sides.

Heat the oil in a cast-iron skillet. Add the steaks and cook over high heat for 3 minutes on each side for medium rare. Remove the steaks and keep warm. Deglaze the pan with the red wine, scraping the bottom. Add the stock and cook over high heat until reduced to ¾ cup. Remove the pan from the heat and stir in the sour cream.

Serve each steak with some of the deglazing sauce, wild rice, and turnips.

Serves 4

◇Steamed Leeks with Crawfish Vinaigrette
◇Brisket of Beef with Stampot

Following the pale green leeks with the pink crawfish, I like this substantial brisket with potatoes and other winter vegetables. The leeks are good hot or cold, so make them whenever it is best for your schedule. Cook the brisket and stampot so they are finished just before dinner, or make them ahead and reheat.

Steamed Leeks with Crawfish Vinaigrette   CAL 172

Pro 9.2 g, Cho 19.1 g, Fat 7.8 g, Sat 0.9 g, Chol 24 mg, Fiber 2.3 g, Ca 145 mg, Zn 0.8 mg, Fe 3.6 mg, Folate 66 mcg, Na 75.5 mg, Suc 0.4 g

Brisket of Beef with Stampot   CAL 516

Pro 38.6 g, Cho 55.4 g, Fat 14.2 g, Sat 5.1 g, Chol 85.7 mg, Fiber 3.4 g, Ca 137.5 mg, Zn 5.5 mg, Fe 8.2 mg, Folate 132.3 mcg, Na 153.6 mg, Suc 8 g

Total Menu   CAL 688

Pro 47.8 g, Cho 74.5 g, Fat 22 g, Sat 6 g, Chol 109.7 mg, Fiber 5.7 g, Ca 282.5 mg, Zn 6.3 mg, Fe 11.8 mg, Folate 198.3 mcg, Na 229.1 mg, Suc 8.4 g

◇Steamed Leeks with Crawfish Vinaigrette

In the onion family, leeks look like overgrown scallions but are much more delicate in flavor. They are fabulous braised in stock or served with this hearty vinaigrette.

Crawfish, also called crayfish, are found in the Deep South, along the southern Atlantic coast, and in the West. Cooked, shelled, and frozen, they are shipped around the country. If you cannot find them, use cooked, chopped shrimp.

1 pound leeks
¼ cup snipped fresh dill
2 jalapeño peppers, cored, seeded, and cut into julienne
½ cup (2 ounces) diced red onion
1 ¼-pound tomato, cut into ¼-inch dice
1 tablespoon chopped cilantro (fresh coriander)
Juice of ½ lemon
2 tablespoons red wine vinegar
2 tablespoons olive oil
½ teaspoon salt-free mustard
¼ pound cooked shelled crawfish

Bring some water to a boil in the bottom of a steamer. Cut the roots and tough top leaves off the leeks. Cut each in half lengthwise and wash well under cold running water. Place on a steamer rack, folded to fit inside. Sprinkle the leeks with the dill and jalapeño. Cover and place over the boiling water. Cook until the leeks are done but still crisp, about 10 minutes.

While the leeks are cooking, prepare the vinaigrette. Put the onion and tomato in a mixing bowl with the cilantro and lemon juice. Stir in the vinegar, oil, mustard, and crawfish. Mix well.

When the leeks are done, cut each half in half crosswise then halve them again lengthwise. If the leeks are very thick, cut each length in half again. Arrange the leeks on 4 salad plates or a platter so they fan out a bit and the tops are folded under. Spoon the vinaigrette on top.

Serve immediately, or cover and leave at room temperature for a few hours.

Serves 4

◇Brisket of Beef with Stampot

Stampot is a Dutch side dish, mostly potatoes, usually flavored with bacon fat. It is excellent with braised beef. This lighter version is equally addicting.

1¼ pounds beef brisket, trimmed of all fat
7 cloves garlic, thinly sliced
1 tablespoon corn oil
¼ cup Beef Stock or water
2 pounds onions, sliced, plus ¼ pound onions, cut into 1-inch
    chunks (1 cup)
Freshly ground black pepper
¼ pound carrots, cut into 1-inch chunks (1 cup)
¼ pound brussels sprouts, cut in half (1 cup)
¼ pound kale, washed and cut into ¼-inch pieces
2 large (2-ounce) stalks celery, cut into ⅛-inch slices
1 jalapeño pepper, cored, seeded, and minced
1 pound potatoes, peeled and cut into 2-inch chunks
1½ cups Chicken Stock or water
⅛ teaspoon freshly grated nutmeg

Preheat the oven to 350° F.

With a small knife, make slits in the meat all over the surface. Push a piece of garlic into each hole. Use about 3 cloves for the brisket, reserving the rest for the stampot. Heat the oil in a 10-inch ovenproof pan. (A heavy skillet with a metal handle and cover does well.) Add the meat and cook over high heat for 5 minutes to brown. Turn with tongs and brown the other side, another 5 minutes. Remove the meat. Add the ¼ cup beef stock or water to the pan. Scrape the bottom of the pan to deglaze.

Add the sliced onions and toss to coat with the stock. Return the meat to the pan over the layer of onions. Cover and place in the oven. Season with pepper. Cook until fork tender, about 2½ hours.

If preparing the meat in advance, cool to room temperature and then refrigerate. Once cold, slice and reheat with the onions before serving. The dish may also be frozen for a few weeks.

The stampot may also be done ahead and reheated. Put all the remaining ingredients, except the nutmeg, into a 3-quart pot. Bring to a boil, cover, and simmer for 45 minutes. Check now and then to be sure the mixture isn't sticking to the bottom of the pot. Uncover and cook at medium high heat until almost all the liquid evaporates, about 10 minutes. Add the nutmeg. Mash the vegetables with a potato masher or wooden spoon to make a lumpy mixture.

Serve the stampot hot with slices of brisket and the onions.

Serves 4

◇Baked Apples
with Red Cabbage
◇Lindstrom Steak

At The Four Seasons, we usually serve the apples with cabbage as a side dish with duck, where they are sometimes overlooked. Here I decided to give them a more prominent role, as a course in themselves. However, if you prefer, serve the apples with their cabbage stuffing alongside the Lindstrom steak smothered in onions.

Baked Apples with Red Cabbage   CAL 192

Pro 3.3 g, Cho 33 g, Fat 4.5 g, Sat 0.4 g, Chol 0 mg, Fiber 2.6 g, Ca 64.2 mg, Zn 0.8 mg, Fe 1.9 mg, Folate 59 mcg, Na 48.7 mg, Suc 5 g

Lindstrom Steak   CAL 426

Pro 34.9 g, Cho 28.1 g, Fat 18.3 g, Sat 5.9 g, Chol 87.9 mg, Fiber 2.6 g, Ca 185.6 mg, Zn 5.8 mg, Fe 9.7 mg, Folate 302.8 mcg, Na 199.7 mg, Suc 4.6 g

Total Menu   CAL 618

Pro 38.2 g, Cho 61.1 g, Fat 22.8 g, Sat 6.3 g, Chol 87.9 mg, Fiber 5.2 g, Ca 249.8 mg, Zn 6.6 mg, Fe 11.6 mg, Folate 361.8 mcg, Na 248.4 mg, Suc 9.6 g

◇Baked Apples with Red Cabbage

Apples and cabbage are paired together in countless dishes. In some, the cabbage dominates, in others, the apple. Here they are on equal footing.

2 Granny Smith or other green apples
1 tablespoon corn oil
¼ cup chopped onion
1 clove garlic, thinly sliced
1 tablespoon minced jalapeño pepper
2 tablespoons red wine vinegar
½ cup dry white wine
½ cup Chicken Stock
½ cup cranberries
1 pound red cabbage, thinly sliced
¼ cup julienned beet
1 1-inch piece cinnamon stick
1 tablespoon honey

Cut the apples in half crosswise. Trim the tops and bottoms so each half can sit flat on your work surface, cut side up. With a melon baller, cut out and discard the seeds. Then cut out enough apple to make an opening 1 inch deep, leaving walls about ⅜ inch thick. Save the trimmings.

Heat the oil in a 2-quart pot. Add the onion, garlic, and jalapeño pepper. Cook for a few minutes until lightly browned. Add the vinegar and scrape the bottom of the pot to deglaze. Add the remaining ingredients with the apple trimmings. Bring to a boil, cover, and cook over medium heat for about 1¼ hours.

Preheat the oven to 375° F.

Divide the cabbage mixture among the apple halves, pressing it firmly into each cavity. Place the stuffed apples in a baking dish and bake for 15 to 20 minutes, or until the apples are tender.

Serves 4

◇Lindstrom Steak

Almost every country makes chopped meat dishes using veal, beef, pork, or combinations. Most often they are formed into meatballs and cooked through, never served rare like American hamburgers. Lindstrom steak is basically a Swedish hamburger flavored with pickled beets, capers, and anchovies.

1 1/4 pounds very lean ground beef
2 anchovies (1/4 ounce) soaked in water for 1 hour to eliminate salt and oil, patted dry, and minced
2 tablespoons capers
1/4 cup pickled beets, cut into 1/4-inch cubes
3/4 cup minced shallots
1/2 cup chopped fresh parsley
1 tablespoon minced jalapeño pepper
Pinch grated nutmeg
2 tablespoons corn oil
4 cups onions, cut into 1/4-inch-thick slices
1/2 cup Beef or Chicken Stock or water
1 pound leaf spinach
1/4 cup dry sherry
1/2 pound mushrooms, sliced
12 cherry tomatoes
Freshly ground black pepper

In a bowl, mix the ground beef with the anchovies, capers, beets, ¼ cup shallots, parsley, jalapeño pepper, and nutmeg. Divide the mixture into 4 parts. Shape each into an oval about 6 inches long and 1½ inches thick.

Heat 1½ teaspoons corn oil in a 10-inch nonstick pan over high heat. Add the onions and cook for a few moments to soften. Add the stock, cover, and cook over low heat for 30 minutes or until the onions are soft and very brown.

While the onions are cooking, prepare the spinach. Bring a large pot of water to a boil. Add the spinach and cook for a minute to blanch. Drain and squeeze dry.

In a separate nonstick pan, heat 1½ teaspoons oil. Add the beef and cook for 3 minutes on a side for rare. Remove from the pan and keep warm. Pour in the sherry and scrape the bottom of the pan to deglaze. Pour the deglazing liquid over the onions.

Heat the remaining tablespoon oil in a skillet. Add the remaining ½ cup shallots and cook until lightly browned, about 3 minutes. Add the mushrooms and sauté until they soften. They should not give off liquid. Add the blanched spinach. Cook just to heat through. Just before serving, add the cherry tomatoes and some black pepper. Toss to gently heat.

To serve, put one Lindstrom steak on a plate; spoon the onions over. Grind black pepper on top. Put some of the spinach and mushrooms on the side.

Serves 4

◇Steamed Vegetables with Lemon Vinaigrette
◇Braised Beefsteak with Beer and Onion

These beautiful, barely steamed vegetables with their lemony sauce pique the appetite for the beef braised in beer with lots of onions, cooked until they are soft and sweet.

Cutting the vegetables takes the most time. If you do it ahead, keep them well chilled until ready to cook. You can make the beef earlier and reheat it, but the kasha is best fresh.

Steamed Vegetables with Lemon Vinaigrette   CAL 166

Pro 4.4 g, Cho 19.6 g, Fat 8 g, Sat 1.1 g, Chol 0 mg, Fiber 2.4 g, Ca 80.4 mg, Zn 1.1 mg, Fe 2.7 mg, Folate 86.5 mcg, Na 58.4 mg, Suc 0.7 g

Braised Beefsteak with Beer and Onion
CAL 457

Pro 33.1 g, Cho 36.1 g, Fat 17.1 g, Sat 6.5 g, Chol 85.9 mg, Fiber 4.3 g, Ca 54.6 mg, Zn 6 mg, Fe 5.3 mg, Folate 62 mcg, Na 75.3 mg, Suc 3.3 g

Total Menu   CAL 623

Pro 37.5 g, Cho 55.7 g, Fat 25.1 g, Sat 7.6 g, Chol 85.9 mg, Fiber 6.7 g, Ca 135 mg, Zn 7.1 mg, Fe 8 mg, Folate 148.5 mcg, Na 133.7 mg, Suc 4 g

◇Steamed Vegetables with Lemon Vinaigrette

I vary the exact vegetables I use for this dish depending on what is available. Look for variety in color and texture.

¼ *pound zucchini*
¼ *pound yellow squash*
¼ *pound turban squash, peeled*
¼ *pound carrots, peeled*
¼ *pound turnips, peeled*
¼ *pound eggplant*
¼ *pound string beans*
Juice of 2 lemons
1 tablespoon salt-free mustard
2 tablespoons olive oil
½ *cup Vegetable Stock*
¼ *cup diced green bell pepper*
¼ *cup diced red bell pepper*
¼ *cup chopped red radishes*
4 scallions, cut into thin rounds
1 bunch chives, chopped
1 2.5-ounce package 2-Mamina (Japanese radish sprouts)

Cut the zucchini, yellow and turban squashes, carrots, turnips, and eggplant attractively into even slices or batonettes, or trim them into rounded, "turned" forms (see page 20). Cut the ends off the string beans and trim them so they are all about the same size.

Bring water to a boil in the bottom of a steamer. Put the vegetables in a steamer basket, cover, and cook over the boiling water until just done, but still crisp, 5 to 10 minutes.

While the vegetables cook, whisk together the lemon juice, mustard, olive oil, and stock. When smooth, stir in the bell peppers, radishes, scallions, and chives.

Remove the vegetables to a serving platter. Put them in piles of each kind, placing them so the colors contrast. Spoon the vinaigrette over the warm vegetables. Garnish with 2-Mamina.

Serves 4

◇Braised Beefsteak with Beer and Onion

This dish is often called Swiss steak, but never in my native Switzerland, where we think of it as carbonnade de boeuf, inspired by Belgium.

4 5-ounce slices beef cross rib, each ½ inch thick
Freshly ground black pepper
1 tablespoon olive oil
2 cloves garlic, sliced
1 jalapeño pepper, cored, seeded, and minced
1 pound onions, sliced crosswise ¼ inch thick
1 cup peeled, seeded, and chopped plum tomatoes
¼ cup water plus 1⅓ cups boiling water
1 12-ounce bottle dark beer
1 bay leaf
⅔ cup whole-grain buckwheat kernels (kasha)

Season the meat with freshly ground black pepper on both sides. Heat the oil in a nonstick skillet. Add half the beef and brown over high heat for 3 minutes on each side. Put the browned beef in a 3-quart casserole. Cook the remaining beef in the skillet. When browned, add to the beef in the casserole.

Put the garlic, jalapeño pepper, onions, and tomatoes in the skillet with ¼ cup water. Cook slowly for about 10 minutes.

Remove the beef from the casserole briefly, leaving behind any juices it has given off. Put a third of the onion mixture into the casserole. Top with a layer of meat, more onion, more beef, the rest of the onion. Stir some beer into the skillet and scrape the bottom with a rubber spatula to deglaze.

Pour the liquid, along with the rest of the beer, into the casserole. Add the bay leaf. Bring the liquid to a boil. Cover, lower the heat, and simmer for about 1½ hours, or until the meat is tender. Remove the cover and cook about 20 minutes longer, until the sauce is thick. Discard the bay leaf.

Put the kasha in a dry, heavy saucepan. Cook, stirring often, until heated through. Turn the heat to low and add the 1⅓ cups boiling water. Cover the pot and cook for 20 minutes, or until the kasha has absorbed all the water.

Serve the meat with its sauce, the kasha on the side.

Serves 4

◇Beef Broth with Soba and Watercress
◇Boiled Beef

This menu consists of one recipe that turns into two courses. The boiled beef, considered by many as an ordinary family dish, is worthy of your finest company when the vegetables, attractively cut, are barely steamed and served with the meat. The meat itself takes a long time to cook—do it ahead so you can get rid of all the fat and have only to reheat everything before serving.

Beef Broth with Soba and Watercress

CAL 29

Pro 1 g, Cho 5.7 g, Fat 0.2 g, Sat 0 g, Chol 0 mg, Fiber 0.1 g, Ca 23.4 mg, Zn 0.2 mg, Fe 0.3 mg, Folate 10.1 mcg, Na 7.3 mg, Suc 0 g

Boiled Beef   CAL 380

Pro 35.6 g, Cho 24.4 g, Fat 16 g, Sat 7.2 g, Chol 101.2 mg, Fiber 2.9 g, Ca 131.1 mg, Zn 6.3 mg, Fe 7 mg, Folate 76 mcg, Na 179 mg, Suc 1.7 g

Total Menu   CAL 409

Pro 36.6 g, Cho 30.1 g, Fat 16.2 g, Sat 7.2 g, Chol 101.2 mg, Fiber 3 g, Ca 154.5 mg, Zn 6.5 mg, Fe 7.3 mg, Folate 86.1 mcg, Na 186.3 mg, Suc 1.7 g

◇Boiled Beef

The by-product of making the boiled beef is the wonderfully rich beef broth you can serve first.

There are many cuts of beef appropriate for boiling, and the names vary from region to region. I like to use the chicken steak, also called tafel-spitz, which is cut from the cross rib.

BEEF

1 medium (¼-pound) onion, skin on, halved

1 1½-pound piece chicken steak, all fat removed

1 medium carrot

4 cloves garlic

1 jalapeño pepper

1 small leek or scallion

1 bunch parsley stems

1 celery stalk

2 bay leaves

6 cloves

¼ nutmeg

1 small (3-ounce) tomato, halved

1 sprig fresh marjoram,
   or ½ teaspoon dried marjoram

1 sprig fresh thyme,
   or ½ teaspoon dried thyme

Peelings from turned vegetables

VEGETABLES

4 1-ounce boiling onions, peeled

¼ pound green cabbage leaves, ribs removed, halved if large

2 ounces peeled parsnip, cut into 4 turned (see page 20) 1½- to
   2-inch pieces

3 ounces peeled carrot, cut into 4 turned 1½- to 2-inch pieces

3 ounces peeled celery root, cut into 4 turned 1½- to 2-inch pieces

1 medium (¼-pound) leek, halved lengthwise, well washed

½ cup fresh Italian parsley leaves

¼ cup grated fresh horseradish

BROTH

1½ ounces soba (Japanese buckwheat noodles), broken into 2-inch
   pieces

2 ounces watercress leaves

Put the onion under a hot broiler and cook, cut side up, until nearly burnt. This will add flavor and color to the beef stock.

Put the beef into a 3-quart pot with hot water to cover. Bring the water to a boil and skim off any scum that rises to the top.

Add the boiling onions and cook for 20 minutes. Remove and set aside with the other vegetables. Add the burnt onion and all the remaining beef ingredients to the pot. Partially cover and simmer until the meat is fork tender, about 2½ hours. Be sure the liquid always barely covers the meat, adding more hot water as necessary. (Cold water will make the liquid cloudy.)

When the meat is almost done, bring some water to a boil in the bottom of a steamer. Line the basket with the cabbage. On top of it put the turned parsnip, carrots, and celery root, along with the leek and boiling onions. Cover and steam for 10 minutes.

When the meat is done, remove it from the pot. Strain the stock, discarding the seasonings and vegetables. Remove any fat from the stock. There should be about 3 cups.

Cut the beef into 8 even slices. Arrange them overlapping along one side of an ovenproof gratin dish. Divide the cabbage into 4 equal piles. Put a fourth of the parsley leaves on top of one pile. Pull the cabbage around the parsley to make a sphere. Wrap it in the corner of a kitchen towel and squeeze to eliminate the moisture and make a small, tight ball. Repeat with the remaining cabbage and parsley. Place the cabbage balls at one end of the gratin dish. Next to them put the turned celery root, then the carrots and parsnips.

Halve each leek half lengthwise to make 4 long pieces. Coil each one around itself, leaving the dark part in the center. Put the leek rolls next to the parsnips and the boiling onions next to them at the end.

Bring a pot of water to a boil. Add the soba and cook until done, about 4 minutes. Drain well. Divide the soba and watercress evenly among 4 small soup bowls.

Spoon ¾ cup reserved stock over the meat and vegetables. Cover with aluminum foil and heat in a 350° F oven for 20 minutes, or until hot. Bring the remaining stock to a boil and spoon it over the soba and watercress for the first course. Have some fresh horseradish available to serve with the meat.

Serves 4

◇Asparagus with Red Pepper Sauce
◇Beef Stew

This is an all-American meal, hearty beef stew dressed up for guests because the vegetables are cooked separately to keep them firm and glistening. The asparagus, with my favorite pepper sauce, are an excellent start to this and many other meals.

Asparagus with Red Pepper Sauce   CAL 113

Pro 5.5 g, Cho 17.9 g, Fat 4.1 g, Sat 0.4 g, Chol 0 mg, Fiber 3.6 g, Ca 53.8 mg, Zn 1.1 mg, Fe 1.9 mg, Folate 112 mcg, Na 21.1 mg, Suc 0.6 g

Beef Stew   CAL 466

Pro 43.4 g, Cho 32 g, Fat 15.1 g, Sat 5.5 g, Chol 101.6 mg, Fiber 3 g, Ca 133.8 mg, Zn 5.8 mg, Fe 8.8 mg, Folate 92.5 mcg, Na 144.8 mg, Suc 2.1 g

Total Menu   CAL 579

Pro 48.9 g, Cho 49.9 g, Fat 19.2 g, Sat 5.9 g, Chol 101.6 mg, Fiber 6.6 g, Ca 187.6 mg, Zn 6.9 mg, Fe 10.7 mg, Folate 204.5 mcg, Na 165.9 mg, Suc 2.7 g

◇Asparagus with Red Pepper Sauce

This is a quick first course that looks wonderful on black or pale green plates. If you should have white asparagus, garnish each plate with green, instead of yellow, pepper.

1¼ pounds trimmed asparagus
1 recipe Red Pepper Puree Sauce (see page 28), heated
1 ½-pound yellow bell pepper, peeled, cored, and seeded, cut into
    ¼-inch dice
Freshly ground black pepper

Heat boiling water in the bottom of a steamer. Put the asparagus in the steamer basket, cover, and cook until done, about 3 minutes.

Spoon some red pepper puree on each of 4 salad plates. Arrange the asparagus neatly on top. Garnish each plate with the diced pepper and a few grindings of black pepper.

Serves 4

◇Beef Stew

Just one of an infinite variety of beef stews, this includes vegetables often overlooked.

1 tablespoon olive oil

1½ pounds beef chuck, all fat removed, cut into 1½-inch cubes

½ cup dry red wine

1 cup chopped onion

1 cup chopped celery

¾ pound tomatoes, peeled, cored, seeded, and cut into 1-inch chunks

2 cloves garlic, minced

1 dried red chili pepper, crumbled

1 cup Beef Stock or salt-free tomato juice

2 bay leaves

½ cup dried white beans, soaked in cold water overnight, drained

3 ounces fennel, cut into ¼-×-¼-×-1½- to 2-inch batonettes

3 ounces peeled carrots, cut into ¼-×-¼-×-1½- to 2-inch batonettes

3 ounces peeled celery root, cut into ¼-×-¼-×-1½- to 2-inch batonettes

3 ounces peeled kohlrabi, cut into ¼-×-¼-×-1½- to 2-inch batonettes

3 ounces peeled rutabaga, cut into ¼-×-¼-×-1½- to 2-inch batonettes

Rind of ½ lemon

1 teaspoon caraway seeds

Heat the oil in a 10-inch nonstick skillet. Add the beef and cook over high heat until browned on all sides. Put the meat in a 3-quart casserole. Pour the red wine into the skillet and scrape the bottom to deglaze. Add the onion, celery, tomatoes, garlic, and chili pepper. Cook for about 5 minutes. Add to the beef with the beef stock, bay leaves, and white beans.

Bring to a boil, then lower the heat, partly cover, and cook until the meat is tender, about 1½ hours.

Put the fennel, carrots, celery root, kohlrabi, and rutabaga in the top of a steamer set over boiling water. Cook until they are done, about 5 minutes.

Grind the lemon rind and caraway seeds together in a spice grinder until very fine. Set aside.

Spoon the stew onto a platter. Arrange the steamed vegetables in a ring around the meat. Sprinkle the lemon-caraway mixture on top.

Serves 4

◇Sliced Summer Fruits with Mango Puree
◇Grilled Beef, Lamb, and Veal Tenderloin with Braised Lentils

This can make an elegant barbecued dinner, easy to serve outside. If you do barbecue, cook the lentils ahead, wrap them in aluminum foil, and reheat on the grill while you cook the vegetables and meat.

Although we offer the summer fruits as a first course at The Four Seasons, you could reverse the order here and make the fruit a very satisfying dessert. If you wish, prepare the platter earlier in the day, cover it with plastic wrap, and refrigerate. Let the fruits come back to room temperature before you serve them.

Sliced Summer Fruits with Mango Puree

CAL 202

Pro 3 g, Cho 39.9 g, Fat 5.7 g, Sat 0.4 g, Chol 0 mg, Fiber 2 g, Ca 48.3 mg, Zn 0.7 mg, Fe 1.3 mg, Folate 57.1 mcg, Na 11.2 mg, Suc 15.1 g

Grilled Beef, Lamb, and Veal Tenderloin with Braised Lentils   CAL 482

Pro 39.2 g, Cho 42.8 g, Fat 14.1 g, Sat 5 g, Chol 81.9 mg, Fiber 3.4 g, Ca 97.1 mg, Zn 5.3 mg, Fe 9 mg, Folate 103.5 mcg, Na 268.7 mg, Suc 1.9 g

Total Menu   CAL 684

Pro 42.2 g, Cho 82.7 g, Fat 19.8 g, Sat 5.4 g, Chol 81.9 mg, Fiber 5.4 g, Ca 145.4 mg, Zn 6 mg, Fe 10.3 mg, Folate 160.6 mcg, Na 279.9 mg, Suc 17 g

◇Sliced Summer Fruits with Mango Puree

I am particularly pleased with the mango puree in this recipe because it cleverly makes use of the fruit around the pits that is often wasted. The bright yellow color makes a sharp contrast to the red of the berries and cherries. As with other recipes using assorted ingredients, these are really suggestions. I vary the platter depending on what is best in that day's market.

2 7-ounce mangoes
Pinch cayenne pepper
Juice of ½ lemon
¼ pound papaya
¼ pound cantaloupe or other melon
¼ pound strawberries
¼ pound cherries
¼ pound peach
¼ pound plum
1 5-ounce orange
¼ pound grapefruit (¼ large)
4 sprigs fresh mint
1 ounce (¼ cup) pecan halves

With a small, sharp knife, cut the peel from the mangoes. With a large knife, cut the pulp away from the pit in 2 cuts per mango, one on each side. This will leave some mango still clinging to the pits. Place a strainer over a bowl and grasp one pit. Scrape it against the strainer to remove all the pulp on both ends. Repeat with the other mango pit. Discard the pits and peels. You should have about ¼ cup puree. Add a pinch of cayenne to it along with the lemon juice. Stir to mix and set aside while you prepare the fruit.

Cut the fruit into attractive shapes. Remove the rind and seeds from the papaya and melon. Cut the flesh into long wedges. Do the same with the mango slices. With a small knife, cut the stems from the strawberries, removing the woody inside as well. Remove the stems from the cherries. If you have a cherry pitter, use it so the cherries stay whole. Otherwise, leave the pits in. Cut the peach and plum into wedges, leaving the skin on, but discarding the pits. Trim the ends off the orange and slice it into even rounds. Cut the rind off the grapefruit with a knife. Cut away whole sections, discarding the membrane.

Spoon the mango puree into the center of a round platter. Arrange the mango, melon, and papaya evenly around, somewhat like spokes on a wheel. Place the peach, plum, grapefruit, and orange between them. Put the strawberries and cherries in the center with the mint and pecans.

Serves 4

◇Grilled Beef, Lamb, and Veal Tenderloin with Braised Lentils

One of the heartiest main courses, this is a simplified version of the British mixed grill. I arrange the three different kinds of grilled tenderloin like petals on a flower. The vegetables, preferably cut into oval pieces like the meat, then fit in between. The braised lentils form the center of the flower, topped by the grilled mushroom cap. Use whatever vegetables are available, including kohlrabi, daikon, other squashes, regular eggplant. If it is difficult to cut them into ovals, make rounds or strips or whatever looks attractive. There should be four pieces of each vegetable.

¼ pound carrot, cut into 4 attractive pieces
6 ounces lamb tenderloin, trimmed of all fat
6 ounces beef tenderloin, trimmed of all fat
6 ounces veal tenderloin, trimmed of all fat
½ teaspoon black peppercorns
½ teaspoon dried rosemary
½ teaspoon dried thyme
½ teaspoon dried sage
¼ pound zucchini, cut into 4 attractive pieces
¼ pound oriental eggplant, cut into 4 attractive pieces
4 fresh shiitake mushroom caps
Juice of 2 limes
1 recipe Braised Lentils (see below)
Freshly ground black pepper

Bring a large pot of water to a boil. Drop in the carrot and cook for 3 minutes, or until almost done. Drain and pat dry.

Cut each piece of tenderloin into 4 even pieces about ¾ inch thick. Grind the peppercorns, rosemary, thyme, and sage together in a spice or coffee grinder until powdery. Rub the mixture onto each piece of meat. Set aside to marinate for an hour or so.

About half an hour before you are ready to serve, heat a grill to hot. Arrange all the carrots, zucchini, eggplant, and mushroom caps on the rack and cook until clearly browned by the grate. Rotate each vegetable (except the mushrooms) 45 degrees and let brown again on the same side. This should give each piece a diamond pattern on the bottom. (This takes a bit of practice, so don't worry if it doesn't work the first time.) Turn the vegetables over and cook on the other side until done through. Remove from the heat, squeeze the lime juice on top, and keep warm.

Place the fillets on the grill and cook them in the same way so each piece is clearly marked with a diamond pattern. It should take about 2 minutes per side to cook the meat until it is done.

Place a portion of the lentils in the center of 4 heated plates and arrange the meat and vegetables as explained in the recipe introduction. Grind black pepper on top of the meat.

If you prefer, put all the meat and vegetables on an oval platter, grouping the meats and vegetables together. Serve the lentils on the side.

If you do not have a grill, use a broiler to cook the fillets and vegetables. If possible, place the meat on a metal grilling rack so the lines of the rack leave a pattern on each piece.

Serves 4

◇Braised Lentils

Lentils are among the fastest-cooking of the dried legumes since they do not need to be soaked first. If you make these ahead, reserve some of the liquid. It will be absorbed in the reheating.

1 tablespoon corn oil
½ clove garlic, minced
½ jalapeño pepper, cored, seeded, and minced
½ cup chopped onions
2 large (2-ounce) stalks celery, chopped
5 ounces (¾ cup) lentils
1½ ounces sun-dried tomatoes, not packed in oil, soaked in warm
  water for ½ hour, drained, and chopped
3 cups Chicken Stock
1½ teaspoons red wine vinegar
⅓ cup chopped fresh parsley

Heat the oil in a 10-inch skillet. Add the garlic, jalapeño pepper, onions, and celery. Sauté for 3 minutes to soften. Add the lentils and tomatoes along with the stock and vinegar. Bring to a boil, then lower the heat so the liquid simmers. Cook, partially covered, for 30 minutes. Uncover and raise the heat. Cook 15 minutes longer. The lentils will be tender. The mixture should be thick, almost all the liquid absorbed. Stir in the parsley.

Serves 4

◇Mushroom Barley Soup
◇Steamed Loin of Pork

Here, again, I have taken liberties with different cuisines, starting with a European soup and going on to a room-temperature loin of pork made with Indian spices. If everything is organized ahead, you'll barely have to go into the kitchen once your guests have arrived.

Mushroom Barley Soup   CAL 280

Pro 13 g, Cho 32.3 g, Fat 6.1 g, Sat 0.8 g, Chol 13.6 mg, Fiber 1.4 g, Ca 53.9 mg, Zn 1.6 mg, Fe 3.4 mg, Folate 25.8 mcg, Na 404 mg, Suc 0.9 g

Steamed Loin of Pork   CAL 363

Pro 31.2 g, Cho 19.9 g, Fat 17.9 g, Sat 5.4 g, Chol 85 mg, Fiber 1.8 g, Ca 109.8 mg, Zn 2.5 mg, Fe 7 mg, Folate 165.7 mcg, Na 86.7 mg, Suc 3.5 g

Total Menu   CAL 643

Pro 44.2 g, Cho 52.2 g, Fat 24 g, Sat 6.2 g, Chol 98.6 mg, Fiber 3.2 g, Ca 163.7 mg, Zn 4.1 mg, Fe 10.4 mg, Folate 191.5 mcg, Na 490.7 mg, Suc 4.4 g

◇Mushroom Barley Soup

Mushroom barley is a warming winter soup in eastern Europe, where mushrooming remains a popular fall activity. Many dry their bounty to preserve it so they can make soups like this during the winter when fresh mushrooms are rarely seen. The taste of dried mushrooms is much more intense than that of cultivated varieties.

1 ounce dried porcini, soaked in cold water to cover for 1 hour
1 tablespoon corn oil
½ cup ¼-inch onion cubes
½ cup ¼-inch celery cubes
½ cup ¼-inch fennel cubes
2 cloves garlic, minced
2 dried red chili peppers
½ cup pearl barley
¼ pound lean ham, diced
1 quart Beef or Vegetable Stock
½ cup ¼-inch peeled parsnip cubes
½ cup ¼-inch peeled carrot cubes
½ cup ¼-inch peeled kohlrabi cubes

When the porcini have soaked enough, drain them and reserve the liquid. There should be about ¾ cup. Roughly chop the porcini and set aside.

Heat the oil in a 3-quart soup pot. Add the onion, celery, fennel, garlic, and chili peppers. Cook for about 2 minutes, until soft but not brown. Add the barley, ham, stock, mushrooms and their liquid with the parsnip, carrot, and kohlrabi. Bring to a boil, lower the heat to a simmer, and cook, partially covered, until everything is soft, about 1½ hours. Discard the chili peppers before serving.

Serves 4

◇Steamed Loin of Pork

The seasonings for the pork are Indian in feeling, tempering the richness of the meat.

1 tablespoon minced fresh ginger
1 tablespoon coriander seed
2 cloves garlic
1 dried red chili pepper
1 bay leaf
1 teaspoon ground turmeric
1 teaspoon Szechuan pepper
1¼ pounds boneless pork tenderloin, trimmed of all fat
2 scallions, cut into ¼-inch rounds
1 teaspoon arrowroot dissolved in 1 tablespoon red wine vinegar
1 tablespoon olive oil
1 large (1-pound) grapefruit
12 large romaine lettuce leaves, ribs removed
20 endive leaves

Put all the seasonings in a spice grinder and grind into a paste. Spread the paste all over the pork.

Put a large piece of plastic wrap on your work surface. Sprinkle half the scallions on the plastic. Cover with the pork. Put the rest of the scallions on top of the pork. Wrap the plastic around the pork to seal. Wrap again with another sheet or two of plastic.

Bring some water in the bottom of a steamer to a boil. Place the pork on the steamer rack, cover, and steam over the boiling water for 30 minutes. Let cool.

Place the pork on a plate with something under part of it so it sits at an angle. With scissors, snip a hole in the plastic so the excess liquid runs out. Catch the liquid and put it in a pot, then bring to a boil. Whisk in the arrowroot-vinegar until smooth, then beat in the oil.

With a knife, cut the rind and all the white pith from the grapefruit, then cut it into its natural sections, discarding the membrane. Set aside.

On a platter, make 4 piles of romaine leaves. Inside them, but extending below, put piles of endive leaves. Put the grapefruit sections over the endives. Cut the pork into very thin slices. Arrange them overlapping on the platter. Sprinkle some of the sauce on the meat, the rest on the salads.

Serves 4

◇Artichoke Stuffed with Pork
◇Steamed Loin of Lamb with Wild Rice

This is one of the more substantial Spa Cuisine meals, sure to satisfy everyone. As usual, the artichoke and lamb can be readied ahead. Start cooking the wild rice first, then the artichokes. Put the lamb in the steamer just before serving the first course. You can return to the kitchen when the lamb is done to make the sauce and arrange the plates.

Artichoke Stuffed with Pork   CAL 231

*Pro 16 g, Cho 30.3 g, Fat 11.3 g, Sat 2.3 g, Chol 24.6 mg, Fiber 5.3 g,
Ca 157.4 mg, Zn 1.8 mg, Fe 4.9 mg, Folate 105.4 mcg, Na 130.6 mg,
Suc 1 g*

Steamed Loin of Lamb with Wild Rice
CAL 441

*Pro 31.5 g, Cho 34 g, Fat 14.2 g, Sat 5.4 g, Chol 81.1 mg, Fiber 1.4 g,
Ca 74.7 mg, Zn 5.2 mg, Fe 6.6 mg, Folate 68.1 mcg, Na 149.7 mg,
Suc 0.4 g*

Total Menu   CAL 672

*Pro 47.5 g, Cho 64.3 g, Fat 25.5 g, Sat 7.7 g, Chol 105.7 mg, Fiber 6.7 g,
Ca 232.1 mg, Zn 7 mg, Fe 11.5 mg, Folate 173.5 mcg, Na 280.3 mg,
Suc 1.4 g*

◇Artichoke Stuffed with Pork

For a light appetizer, I use only the artichoke bottom. In this case, I wanted something more substantial.

4 7-ounce artichokes (about 3½ inches in diameter)
2 tablespoons olive oil
½ cup minced onions
1 tablespoon minced jalapeño pepper
1 cup minced fennel
5 ounces pork tenderloin, trimmed of all fat, minced
3 tablespoons minced dried porcini, soaked in water to cover for 1
   hour
1 tablespoon chopped sun-dried tomato, not packed in oil, soaked
   with the porcini
¼ teaspoon ground mace
¼ teaspoon freshly grated nutmeg
¼ cup whole-wheat bread crumbs
¼ cup water

Preheat the oven to 350° F.

With a paring knife, cut away the outer layer of the artichoke stems until the paler flesh shows. Working with one artichoke at a time, begin by tearing off the inedible outer leaves, peeling them away from the artichoke. After you have removed a few rows, break the leaves in half, approximately, so the thick bottom remains attached. With a paring knife, trim away any hard parts of the leaves still attached so everything left is edible. With a spoon, pull out and discard the center chokes. The center should be about $1\frac{1}{4}$ inches deep.

Heat 1 tablespoon oil in a small iron skillet. Add the onions and jalapéno pepper. Sauté until lightly browned, about 2 minutes. Add the fennel and cook 2 minutes longer. Add the pork and cook 2 minutes more. Put the mixture into a mixing bowl with the porcini, tomato, ground mace, nutmeg, and bread crumbs.

Divide the mixture in 4 and stuff one part into each artichoke, pressing it firmly into the opening. Put the remaining tablespoon oil in the bottom of an ovenproof casserole with a tight-fitting lid just large enough to hold the 4 artichokes. Place the artichokes in the casserole, stems up. Pour in the water. Bring to a boil over medium heat, then cover and bake for 30 minutes, or until the artichokes are tender. Check after 15 minutes and add a little more liquid if necessary.

Remove carefully from the pot and serve one to each guest, stem up.

Serves 4

◇Steamed Loin of Lamb with Wild Rice

The cabbage leaves make an attractive casing for the lamb, keeping it moist and adding flavor at the same time.

2 8-ounce pieces lamb tenderloin, trimmed of all fat
¼ teaspoon ground coriander
¼ teaspoon ground cumin
1 clove garlic, minced
Juice of ½ lemon
Freshly ground black pepper
Savoy cabbage
4 scallions
2 cups Lamb Stock, reduced to ¾ cup
1 tablespoon unsalted butter
1 recipe Wild Rice (see page 90)

Rub each lamb fillet with half the coriander, cumin, garlic, and lemon juice. Grind black pepper over all sides. Set aside to marinate for 2 to 3 hours at room temperature, or refrigerate overnight.

Bring a large pot of water to the boil. Pull off and discard the hard, very dark outer cabbage leaves. Cut out the core and pull the leaves off one by one. You'll need about twelve (6 ounces). Put them in the boiling water to soften, about 2 minutes. Drain them under cold running water. Put the scallions in the same water to blanch, about 2 minutes. Drain under cold water. Cut each in half crosswise. Cut away the roots.

Spread a kitchen towel on your work surface. Trim the center veins on the cabbage leaves so they lie flat (do not cut them out). Using the dark leaves first, arrange 2 leaves on the towel so the core ends meet in the middle and they slightly overlap. Place whole or half lighter cabbage leaves over them so you have a solid rectangle about 10 inches long and 9 inches wide. Put 2 blanched scallion greens on the cabbage going the long way.

Put one lamb fillet over the scallions to cover. Top with 2 scallion whites, going in the same direction. Fold the short ends of cabbage over the lamb and roll up like an egg roll. Place on a 20-inch piece of good-quality plastic wrap. Fold over to seal. Tuck in the ends and wrap in another piece of plastic in the other direction. (This is easiest if you have someone to help who can keep the plastic taut as you work.) Repeat with the other lamb fillet and remaining scallions and cabbage. Place the rolled lamb fillets on a steamer rack.

Bring some of the cabbage water to a boil in the bottom of a wok or steamer. Cover the steamer rack and place it over the boiling water. Steam for 10 minutes. Let the lamb rest for 5 minutes, still covered.

Meanwhile, heat the stock and whisk in the butter. Season to taste with freshly ground black pepper.

Remove the plastic from the lamb rolls. Cut off the ends so they are even. Slice each roll into 6 pieces, about ¾ inch wide. Serve 3 slices per person on a plate with some of the sauce and wild rice.

Serves 4

◇Grated Raw Vegetable Salads
◇Fillet of Spring Lamb with Kasha

Make this meal when spring lamb comes to market along with fine new carrots and cucumbers. All the salads and the eggplant sauce can be made ahead while the lamb marinates. The cooking of the string beans and kasha is largely unattended, leaving you to watch over the lamb. If you can't get the exact greens called for, feel free to substitute, but try to have as much contrast in color as possible.

Grated Raw Vegetable Salads   CAL 158

*Pro 6.1 g, Cho 24.5 g, Fat 5.9 g, Sat 0.7 g, Chol 0.8 mg, Fiber 2.2 g, Ca
178.5 mg, Zn 1.9 mg, Fe 4.6 mg, Folate 150.4 mcg, Na 92.7 mg,
Suc 0.6 g*

Fillet of Spring Lamb with Kasha   CAL 466

*Pro 35.5 g, Cho 42.3 g, Fat 15.1 g, Sat 4.6 g, Chol 91.3 mg, Fiber 3.1 g,
Ca 73.1 mg, Zn 4.2 mg, Fe 5.1 mg, Folate 61.6 mcg, Na 236.3 mg,
Suc 0.7 g*

Total Menu   CAL 624

*Pro 41.6 g, Cho 66.8 g, Fat 21 g, Sat 5.3 g, Chol 92.1 mg, Fiber 5.3 g,
Ca 251.6 mg, Zn 6.1 mg, Fe 9.7 mg, Folate 212 mcg, Na 329 mg,
Suc 1.3 g*

◇Grated Raw Vegetable Salads

In Switzerland, a plate of assorted salads like this is typically found in tea rooms, where it is called *damen teller*, "ladies' plate."

CARROT SALAD

¼ *cup raisins, soaked in water for 1 hour*
1 cup shredded carrots
Juice of ¼ lemon
2 tablespoons coarsely chopped walnuts
¼ *cup unflavored low-fat yogurt*
Freshly ground black pepper

BEET SALAD

¼ *pound beets*
2 shallots, thinly sliced
1 teaspoon balsamic vinegar
1 teaspoon corn oil
Freshly ground black pepper

JICAMA SALAD

1 cup (5 ounces) shredded jicama or red radish
¼ *cup chopped fresh chives*
1 teaspoon fresh lemon juice
Freshly ground pepper

CUCUMBER SALAD

1 cup shredded peeled cucumber
¼ *cup chopped fresh dill*
1 teaspoon white wine vinegar
1 teaspoon olive oil
Freshly ground black pepper, or 1 teaspoon minced jalapeño

8 radicchio leaves

4 Boston lettuce leaves

2 ounces endive

2 ounces small spinach leaves

¼ pound chopped mushrooms

1 2.5-ounce package 2-Mamina (Japanese radish sprouts)

Carrot salad: Drain the raisins. Put them in a bowl with the carrots, lemon juice, walnuts, and yogurt. Mix well. Add black pepper to taste.

Beet salad: Drop the beets into a pot of boiling water. Cook until a skewer can just get through, but the beets are still firm. Drain and cool, then peel and shred. Put in a bowl with the shallot slices, vinegar, and corn oil. Season to taste with black pepper.

Jicama salad: Squeeze the jicama to remove any liquid given off in the shredding. Toss it with the chives, lemon juice, and pepper to taste.

Cucumber salad: Squeeze the cucumber to eliminate excess liquid. Mix it with the dill, vinegar, oil, and pepper.

Arrange each plate as follows: Cup the radicchio leaves and fill with the jicama salad. Next to that put the Boston leaves filled with beet salad. Separate the endive into leaves. Spread them out next to the beet salad. Spoon the carrot salad over the endives. To finish the circle, make a bed of spinach leaves and top with the cucumber salad. Put the chopped mushrooms in the center of the plate with the 2-Mamina over them.

Serves 4

◇Fillet of Spring Lamb with Kasha

This very simple sauce has a wonderful flavor.

4 5-ounce lamb fillets
2 tablespoons olive oil
Juice of 2 lemons
½ cup chopped onion
2 cloves minced garlic
1 dried red chili pepper, crumbled
2 teaspoons fresh rosemary, or 1 teaspoon dried rosemary
½ pound eggplant (preferably oriental)
2 cups Lamb Stock
6 ounces (1 cup) whole-grain buckwheat kernels (kasha)
2 cups boiling water
¾ pound string beans

Put the lamb in a shallow pan. Rub with the olive oil, lemon juice, onion, garlic, chili pepper, and rosemary. Set aside to marinate for a few hours at room temperature or refrigerate overnight.

Preheat the oven to 400° F. Wrap the eggplant in foil and bake for 1 hour, or until completely soft and collapsed. Set aside to cool a bit.

Cut the eggplant in half lengthwise. Using a spoon, scrape all the pulp away from the skin. Discard the skin. Put the pulp in a saucepan with the stock. Bring to a boil and simmer, uncovered, until the stock is reduced to ½ cup. Let it cool a bit, then puree the mixture in a food processor or blender. Return to the saucepan to reheat before using.

Preheat the broiler until hot.

Put the kasha in a dry, heavy saucepan. Cook, stirring often, until heated through. Turn the heat to low and add the boiling water. Cover the pot and let cook for 10 minutes, or until the kasha has absorbed all the water.

Bring some water to a boil in the bottom of a steamer. Put the string beans on a steamer rack, cover, and cook until done but still firm, about 5 minutes.

Drain the lamb, reserving the marinade. Put the lamb on a broiler pan and cook under the broiler for 5 minutes. Turn each piece with tongs and cook 5 minutes longer. Set aside and keep warm.

Add the marinade to the eggplant sauce and heat through. Spoon some of the sauce in a pool toward the top of each of 4 heated dinner plates. Cut each piece of lamb on the diagonal into 3 slices. Overlap them in the center of the sauce. Arrange half the string beans to one side of the lamb and half on the other side with the kasha in between, below the lamb.

Serves 4

FILLET OF SPRING LAMB WITH KASHA

263

◇Buckwheat Noodles with Wild Mushrooms
◇Medallions of Lamb with Zucchini and Eggplant

If you prepare all the ingredients and cook the eggplant-and-zucchini mixture ahead, the final cooking times will be brief.

Buckwheat Noodles with Wild Mushrooms   CAL 260

Pro 9.1 g, Cho 39.7 g, Fat 7.7 g, Sat 2.3 g, Chol 8.5 mg, Fiber 1.5 g, Ca 91.1 mg, Zn 1 mg, Fe 3 mg, Folate 81.4 mcg, Na 35.7 mg, Suc 0 g

Medallions of Lamb with Zucchini and Eggplant   CAL 278

Pro 28.9 g, Cho 14.7 g, Fat 12 g, Sat 4.5 g, Chol 93.1 mg, Fiber 1.9 g, Ca 47.2 mg, Zn 4.3 mg, Fe 3.4 mg, Folate 60.9 mcg, Na 74.6 mg, Suc 1.2 g

Total Menu   CAL 538

Pro 38 g, Cho 54.4 g, Fat 19.7 g, Sat 6.8 g, Chol 101.6 mg, Fiber 3.4 g, Ca 138.3 mg, Zn 5.3 mg, Fe 6.4 mg, Folate 142.3 mcg, Na 110.3 mg, Suc 1.2 g

◇Buckwheat Noodles with Wild Mushrooms

Mushrooms and noodles seem to have a natural affinity for each other. They are particularly interesting when the noodles are as full-flavored as these and the mushrooms are fresh from the woods.

6 ounces cha soba (Japanese green tea buckwheat noodles)
1 tablespoon corn oil
3 ounces shallots, chopped
1 clove garlic, minced
1 tablespoon minced jalapeño pepper
¾ pound mixed wild mushrooms, roughly chopped if large
1 ounce mixed fresh herbs (parsley, chervil, tarragon, savory), chopped
¼ pound savoy cabbage, shredded
Freshly ground black pepper
6 tablespoons low-fat sour cream
1 2.5-ounce package 2-Mamina (Japanese radish sprouts)

Bring a large pot of water to a boil. Add the noodles and cook until barely done, about 4 minutes. Drain well.

While the noodles are cooking, heat the oil in a nonstick skillet. Add the shallots, garlic, and jalapeño pepper. Cook until lightly browned. Add the mushrooms, herbs, and cabbage. Cook, tossing, until the mushrooms and cabbage soften. Season with black pepper and stir in the sour cream. Leave it so a little sour cream shows.

Toss the mushroom sauce with the drained noodles. Garnish each plate with a small bunch of 2-Mamina.

Serves 4

◇Medallions of Lamb with Zucchini and Eggplant

There are myriad ways to combine lamb with eggplant, zucchini, and tomato. This is a particularly nice one; the vegetables form a sort of ratatouille.

½ teaspoon coriander seed

1 teaspoon black peppercorns

½ teaspoon dried rosemary

Juice of 1 lemon

1¼ pounds fat-free lamb tenderloin, cut into 12 even slices

1 tablespoon plus 1 teaspoon olive oil

1 medium (5-ounce) red onion, thinly sliced

1 tablespoon minced jalapeño pepper

1 large clove garlic, minced

¼ pound eggplant, cut into 1-inch chunks

¼ pound tomato, peeled, cored, seeded, and cut into 1-inch chunks

½ pound zucchini, cut into 1-inch chunks

¼ pound green bell pepper, cored, seeded, and cut into 1-inch squares

¼ pound red bell pepper, cored, seeded, and cut into 1-inch squares

1 teaspoon fresh oregano, or ¼ teaspoon dried oregano

Grind the coriander, black peppercorns, and rosemary together in a spice or coffee grinder until powdery. Squeeze the lemon juice over the lamb, then spread each piece with some of the spice mixture. Set aside to marinate for a few hours.

Heat 1 tablespoon oil in a 10-inch nonstick skillet. Add the onion, jalapeño pepper, and garlic. Sauté over high heat for 2 minutes. Add the vegetables and oregano. (If the mixture seems too dry, add a little water.) Cover the pan, lower the heat, and cook until done, 15 to 18 minutes. If cooked ahead, keep warm.

Just before you are ready to serve, heat the remaining teaspoon oil in a nonstick pan. Add the lamb in a single layer and cook for 30 seconds a side for rare. It will probably be necessary to cook it in 2 batches. Keep the first batch warm as the rest cooks.

Arrange the lamb overlapping down one side of a platter and the eggplant and zucchini on the other side.

Serves 4

NOTE: If you prefer, you can grill the lamb. Lightly oil the grill so the meat doesn't stick. Sear each piece, then rotate it 45 degrees and return to the grill, same side down. This will give it a diamond pattern. Turn over and cook briefly on the other side. Serve with the seared side up.

◇Seafood Aspic
◇Roast Saddle
of Baby Lamb

This is a perfect spring dinner when you want to serve an impressive meal without being tied to the kitchen. The aspic, bits of seafood suspended in glistening stock, needs to be done ahead. I recommend making it the day before. Soak the mushrooms and tomatoes for the rice early in the day, then set everything in the saucepan, ready to start cooking about an hour before you want to eat it. Put the lamb in just before serving the aspic, finishing it in the kitchen when you clear the first course.

Seafood Aspic   CAL 194

Pro 15.2 g, Cho 13.3 g, Fat 7 g, Sat 1.2 g, Chol 45.8 mg, Fiber 2.5 g, Ca 49.7 mg, Zn 1.3 mg, Fe 2.6 mg, Folate 50.1 mcg, Na 219.3 mg, Suc 0 g

Roast Saddle of Baby Lamb   CAL 543

Pro 25.7 g, Cho 59.9 g, Fat 16.8 g, Sat 4.7 g, Chol 63.1 mg, Fiber 1.4 g, Ca 66.2 mg, Zn 4.2 mg, Fe 4.4 mg, Folate 53.5 mcg, Na 140 mg, Suc 4.4 g

Total Menu · CAL 737

Pro 40.9 g, Cho 73.2 g, Fat 23.8 g, Sat 5.9 g, Chol 108.9 mg, Fiber 3.9 g, Ca 115.9 mg, Zn 5.5 mg, Fe 7 mg, Folate 103.6 mcg, Na 359.3 mg, Suc 4.4 g

◇Seafood Aspic

This particular recipe uses sole, striped bass, and shrimp. In the restaurant, I might use lobster, trout, or any other available seafood. The olives are a bit of a surprise.

2½ ounces skinless sole fillet
2½ ounces skinless striped bass fillet
¼ pound shelled, deveined shrimp
4 black olives (1 ounce, weighed with pits)
2 or 3 romaine lettuce leaves
1½ teaspoons julienned lemon rind
1½ teaspoons julienned jalapeño pepper
1½ teaspoons julienned fresh ginger
2 cups Fish Stock, reduced to 1 cup
Unflavored gelatin (optional)
½ recipe Roasted Peppers as prepared for the Roasted Peppers,
    Buckwheat Noodles, and Chicken Salad (see page 116)
1 2.5-ounce package 2-Mamina (Japanese radish sprouts)

Cut the sole and bass into relatively even pieces up to 1½ inches wide and ¾ inch long. Cut the shrimp into ½-inch cubes. Quarter and pit the olives. Cut each quarter in half crosswise.

Bring water to a boil in the bottom of a steamer. Line the steamer basket with the lettuce leaves. They will keep the fish from sticking. Arrange the sole, bass, and shrimp in a layer on the basket. Sprinkle the julienned lemon rind, jalapeño, and ginger on top. Cover and place over the boiling water. Steam for 2 minutes. Set aside to cool.

The fish stock must gel when chilled. To test for its gelling ability, fill a bowl with ice and some cold water. Sprinkle salt on the ice to make the ice colder. Put a spoonful of stock in a ramekin or metal bowl and place it on the iced water. It should become solid but not rubbery when it chills. If the stock is not gelatinous enough, dissolve some unflavored gelatin in a little hot stock. Add to the reduced stock and test again.

When the stock is the right consistency, spoon a thin (⅛-inch) layer into the bottom of each of four 7-ounce flan cups or one 3- to 4-cup wide serving bowl. Place over the iced water to set the stock. Spoon the cooked seafood and seasonings into each cup. Add an equal portion of olives. Pour the remaining stock over the fish. If possible, set a matching cup over each filled one to weight the aspic a bit. Set in the refrigerator at least 2 hours, or until set. The lettuce leaves lining the steamer are not needed for this dish, but they make a delicious (and healthy snack).

To serve, dip the bottom of each mold in hot water for a moment to loosen. Unmold each onto the center of a salad plate. Arrange a portion of the roasted peppers and some 2-Mamina around the aspic.

Serves 4

◇Roast Saddle of Baby Lamb

This is a festive dish to make for Easter. The same method can be used with saddle of baby goat, rabbit, and venison.

Freshly ground black pepper
1 saddle of baby lamb, fillets and all fat removed, about 18 ounces
   trimmed weight
1 teaspoon paprika
1 tablespoon olive oil
1 clove garlic, minced
½ teaspoon ground coriander seed
2 teaspoons whole-wheat bread or cracker crumbs
1 tablespoon chopped fresh parsley
1½ teaspoons fresh tarragon
1½ teaspoons fresh mint leaves
½ jalapeño pepper, cored and seeded
1 teaspoon mustard seeds
1 recipe Brown Rice (see below)
2 cups Lamb Stock, reduced to ¾ cup

Preheat the oven to 400° F.

Grind black pepper over the lamb, then sprinkle the paprika on the top. Rub it in along with the olive oil, garlic, and coriander. Place the meat in a roasting pan. Cook in the preheated oven for 20 minutes. The lamb will be pink.

While the meat cooks (or before), chop together into a fine powder (with a knife or in a food processor) the bread crumbs, parsley, tarragon, mint, and jalapeño pepper. Add the whole mustard seeds.

When the meat has roasted for 20 minutes, remove it from the oven and spread the bread crumb mixture on top. Return to the oven and cook 5 minutes longer to make a crisp coating.

Let the lamb rest for a few minutes, then carve as follows: Cut down on either side of the bone to loosen the meat. With your knife parallel to the cutting board, cut each loin into thin slices. Serve with the brown rice. Use the reduced stock for the sauce.

Serves 4

◇Brown Rice

Brown rice is the whole grain with all the original nutrients. More flavorful than the less nutritious white rice, it is a fine complement to the lamb in this menu, especially when flavored with the sun-dried tomatoes and porcini.

¼ cup dried porcini
¼ cup sun-dried tomatoes, not packed in oil
½ cup water
1 tablespoon olive oil
½ cup diced onion
½ cup diced celery
2 cloves garlic, minced
½ large jalapeño pepper, cored, seeded, and minced
½ pound (1¼ cups) brown rice
1½ cups Chicken Stock
1 cup orange juice
1 bay leaf

Place the porcini and sun-dried tomatoes in a bowl. Add the water and leave to soak for 1 hour. Drain, reserving the liquid, and cut into ¼-inch pieces. Set aside.

Heat the olive oil in a 2-quart saucepan. Add the onion, celery, garlic, and jalapeño pepper. Sauté until lightly browned, about 3 minutes. Add the rice and toss to coat. Add the chopped porcini and tomatoes with their liquid, the chicken stock, orange juice, and bay leaf.

Bring the liquid to a boil, cover, and lower the heat until the liquid just simmers. Cook until the rice is tender, 45 minutes to 1 hour. Discard the bay leaf.

Serves 4

◇Stuffed Red Pepper with Shrimp
◇Sautéed Breast of Quail with Melon on Pecan Rice

The bright red peppers are followed by the orange melon, purple grapes, and browned meat. For this wonderful company dinner, you can stuff the peppers ahead; the rice will cook unattended. The quail will be done in less time than it takes someone else to clear the table.

Stuffed Red Pepper with Shrimp   CAL 222

Pro 12.4 g, Cho 25.8 g, Fat 8.2 g, Sat 2.7 g, Chol 50 mg, Fiber 2.6 g, Ca 76.7 mg, Zn 1.3 mg, Fe 2.2 mg, Folate 50.5 mcg, Na 86.5 mg, Suc 1.7 g

Sautéed Breast of Quail with Melon on Pecan Rice   CAL 339

Pro 13 g, Cho 41.6 g, Fat 12.6 g, Sat 1.7 g, Chol 22.9 g, Fiber 3.4 g, Ca 68.9 mg, Zn 2.2 mg, Fe 3.4 mg, Folate 57.7 mcg, Na 292 mg, Suc 5.4 g

Total Menu   CAL 561

Pro 25.4 g, Cho 67.4 g, Fat 20.8 g, Sat 4.4 g, Chol 72.9 mg, Fiber 6 g, Ca 145.6 mg, Zn 3.5 mg, Fe 5.6 mg, Folate 108.2 mcg, Na 378.5 mg, Suc 7.1 g

◇Stuffed Red Pepper with Shrimp

Kasha is a wonderful, nutty-tasting grain, popular in eastern Europe. It is sold whole, coarse, medium, and fine. The whole not only has the most nutrition, it tastes the best.

1/3 cup whole-grain buckwheat kernels (kasha)
2/3 cup boiling water
4 3 1/2-ounce red bell peppers
1 tablespoon olive oil
1 clove garlic, minced
1 jalapeño pepper, cored, seeded, and minced
1 cup (1/4 pound) minced onion
2/3 cup (2 ounces) diced celery
1 cup (3 1/2 ounces) diced mushrooms
6 ounces shelled, deveined shrimp, cut into 1/3-inch pieces
1/2 cup low-fat sour cream
1/4 cup Chicken Stock or water

Put the kasha in a dry, heavy saucepan. Cook, stirring often, until heated through. Turn the heat to low and add the boiling water. Cover the pot and cook for 10 minutes, or until the kasha has absorbed all the water. Set aside in a mixing bowl.

Preheat the oven to 375° F.

In even pieces, cut the tops off the peppers. Cut out and discard each core, leaving pepper rings. Remove and discard the seeds and ribs from the peppers, being careful not to break them.

Heat the oil in an 8-inch nonstick skillet. Add the garlic, jalapeño pepper, onion, and celery. Cook until lightly browned, 2 to 3 minutes. Add the mushrooms and cook 2 minutes longer. Add the shrimp and cook for another 30 seconds. The shrimp will finish cooking in the oven. Add the shrimp and vegetables to the kasha along with the sour cream. Mix well.

Divide the kasha mixture among the 4 peppers. They should be quite full. Replace each pepper ring top. Place them in a 2½-quart ovenproof casserole that will just hold the peppers firmly in place. Pour the stock or water in the bottom. Bring to a boil on top of the stove, cover, and bake in the preheated oven for 30 minutes. Remove the cover and cook 15 minutes longer.

Serves 4

◇Sautéed Breast of Quail with Melon on Pecan Rice

Tiny quail are tasty, but whole birds are difficult to eat with a knife and fork. I often save our guests the struggle by just serving the breasts. Here, the sweetness of the fruit goes well with the spicy meat and gives the plate extra color.

8 ¼-pound quail
1 ¼-pound carrot, quartered
1 large (2-ounce) stalk celery, halved
1 ¼-pound onion, halved
1 clove garlic
1 bay leaf
1 dried red chili pepper
12 juniper berries
1 tablespoon coriander seed
2 teaspoons Szechuan pepper
½ 20-ounce cranshaw melon
2 teaspoons safflower oil
¼ pound red grapes, stems removed
1 recipe Pecan Rice (see page 42)

With a small, sharp knife, cut the breast pieces off each quail, scraping against the breast bone as you cut. Pull off and discard the skin. Put the breast pieces to one side. Put the carcasses in a 4-quart pot with the carrot, celery, onion, garlic, and bay leaf. Add water just to cover. Bring to a boil and simmer, uncovered, for 2 hours. Skim and remove any fat and scum that rise to the surface.

Put the chili pepper, juniper, coriander seed, and Szechuan pepper in a coffee or spice grinder and grind to a fine powder. Sprinkle about a third of it onto the quail so it evenly covers all sides. Reserve the remaining spice mixture to season lamb, chicken, or veal in another dish. Cover the quail and set aside for a few hours at room temperature or refrigerate overnight.

When the quail stock has cooked for 2 hours, strain it and discard the solids. Return the liquid to a clean saucepan, remove any fat, and boil until reduced to ½ cup.

When ready to serve, preheat the oven to 300° F.

Cut the rind from the melon and scoop out and discard the seeds. Cut the melon into 8 even wedges. Put them on a baking sheet and place in the oven for 3 minutes, or until heated through. Do not let the melon brown.

Heat the safflower oil in a 10-inch nonstick skillet. Add the quail in a single layer and cook for 1 minute. Turn each piece and add the grapes. Cook a minute or so longer. The quail will be rare.

On each of 4 dinner plates, arrange 2 melon pieces so they follow the curve of the plate and face each other. Spoon some of the rice in the center. Arrange the quail over the rice toward the top of the plate and the grapes in a pile toward the bottom. Spoon some of the reduced stock over the rice and quail.

Serves 4

◇Turban of Trout with Avocado
◇Quail Pot au Feu

You can make the guacamole and stuff the trout ahead, then steam it while you make the pot au feu.

Turban of Trout with Avocado   CAL 296

Pro 25.4 g, Cho 3.9 g, Fat 19.9 g, Sat 4.7 g, Chol 62.4 mg, Fiber 0.8 g, Ca 36.2 mg, Zn 1.2 mg, Fe 1.3 mg, Folate 33.4 mcg, Na 95.3 mg, Suc 0.2 g

Quail Pot au Feu   CAL 259

Pro 21.1 g, Cho 19.5 g, Fat 4.9 g, Sat 1.1 g, Chol 45.8 mg, Fiber 2.2 g, Ca 74 mg, Zn 1.4 mg, Fe 3.6 mg, Folate 67.4 mcg, Na 285.2 mg, Suc 0 g

Total Menu   CAL 555

Pro 46.5 g, Cho 23.4 g, Fat 24.8 g, Sat 5.8 g, Chol 108.2 mg, Fiber 3 g, Ca 110.2 mg, Zn 2.6 mg, Fe 4.9 mg, Folate 100.8 mcg, Na 380.5 mg, Suc 0.2 g

◇Turban of Trout
with Avocado

This is one of the simplest recipes I know. The firm flesh of the trout makes a perfect casing for the guacamole, contrasting in color, texture, and taste. For a main course, I serve two turbans with some Pecan Rice (see page 42).

Freshly ground white pepper
4 ¼-pound skinless rainbow trout fillets
Fresh lemon juice
1 recipe Guacamole (see below)

Grind white pepper on each trout fillet and sprinkle on some lemon juice. Make a ring of each fillet, skinned side in, and place one in each of four ½-cup ramekins. Spoon a fourth of the guacamole into each ramekin. Squeeze some lemon juice on top.

Bring water to a boil in the bottom of a steamer. Place the ramekins on the rack, cover, and cook for 10 minutes. Remove from the heat and run a knife around the edge of each ramekin to loosen the fish. Quickly unmold it into your hand and set it, right side up, on a heated salad plate. Repeat with the other ramekins. Serve hot.

Serves 4

◇Guacamole

Guacamole is a wonderful spread, providing the avocados are fully ripe and buttery. They should yield to the touch but not rattle when shaken (that means they are so ripe, the pit is loose). Unripe avocados will continue to develop on your counter. The easiest way to judge ripeness is to look for the rough, thin-skinned Haas avocados. These turn black when they are ready.

1 small avocado
3 tablespoons minced red onion
3 tablespoons ¼-inch red bell pepper cubes
3 tablespoons ¼-inch green bell pepper cubes
3 tablespoons ¼-inch tomato cubes
1½ teaspoons minced jalapeño pepper
1½ packed teaspoons chopped cilantro (fresh coriander)
½ teaspoon fresh lemon juice
1½ teaspoons olive oil
½ teaspoon red wine vinegar
Freshly ground black pepper

With a spoon, scoop the avocado pulp into a bowl. Discard the rind. Add all the remaining ingredients to the bowl.

The best tool for mixing is a clean 8-ounce or 1-pound can, top and bottom removed. Tuna or tomato cans work well. Use the can to chop everything until it is well mixed but still lumpy.

Makes 1 generous cup

◇Quail Pot au Feu

Almost every culture has a tradition of a simple meal of meats and vegetables boiled together in a single pot. The French call it pot au feu; in Italy, it's bollito misto, and in New England, it is the boiled dinner. When we serve pot au feu at The Four Seasons, it is an elegant dish. This one, made with tiny quail in pieces the same size as the vegetables, is far from its humble origins. If you can't get these delicious little birds, look to chicken, pheasant, or Cornish hens. Use only the breast meat and cut it into small pieces to match the vegetables.

8 ¼-pound quail
2 medium carrots
1 ½ large stalks (3 ounces) celery
3 small turnips
6 ounces new potatoes
3 ounces celery root
1 quart Chicken Stock
1 cup (5½ ounces) peas
½ cup thinly sliced scallions
Packed ¼ cup watercress leaves
1 tablespoon minced jalapeño pepper
1 teaspoon minced fresh ginger

Cut the wings off the quail along with the lower leg bones, if they are there. Add these to your next batch of chicken stock.

Cut all the vegetables attractively since they will float in the soup. Peel the carrot and shape it into ¼-inch scalloped rounds. Slice the celery on the diagonal into long pieces about ¼ inch wide. Peel and cut the turnips, potatoes, and celery root into attractive "turned" pieces (see page 20) with curved edges, each about 1½ inches long.

Bring the stock to a boil in a 3-quart pot. Add the carrots, celery, celery root, turnips, and potatoes along with the quail. Let simmer for 8 minutes.

Remove the quail to a plate and let cool a bit. Let the vegetables continue cooking until they are barely done, about 12 minutes longer.

With a small knife and your fingers, pull the breast pieces off the cooked quail; discard the skin. Cut away the leg and thigh meat in single pieces. Set aside. Discard the remaining bones.

When the vegetables are done, add the peas to the pot along with the cooked quail meat. Cook for about 2 minutes to heat through.

Place the scallions, watercress, jalapeño pepper, and ginger in the bottom of a soup tureen. Spoon the hot soup into the tureen. Stir to mix in the ingredients on the bottom.

Serves 4

◇Stuffed Onion
◇Grilled Breast of Pigeon
with Red Wine Sauce

The translucent onion stuffed with dark green spinach leads to the pigeon bathed in its rich mahogany sauce. Stuff the onion ahead, timing the baking to finish at the dinner hour. Prepare the pigeon sauce ahead, leaving only the quick cooking of the breasts at the end.

Stuffed Onion   CAL 135

Pro 7.3 g, Cho 23.6 g, Fat 0.8 g, Sat 0 g, Chol 0.2 mg, Fiber 2.1 g, Ca 124.3 mg, Zn 1.2 mg, Fe 4.6 mg, Folate 222.5 mcg, Na 98.9 mg, Suc 5 g

Grilled Breast of Pigeon with Red Wine Sauce   CAL 535

Pro 30.7 g, Cho 35.3 g, Fat 24.5 g, Sat 7.6 g, Chol 87.4 mg, Fiber 3.1 g, Ca 73.5 mg, Zn 4.2 mg, Fe 5.7 mg, Folate 59.8 mcg, Na 130.7 mg, Suc 1.2 g

Total Menu   CAL 670

Pro 38 g, Cho 58.9 g, Fat 25.3 g, Sat 7.6 g, Chol 87.6 mg, Fiber 5.2 g, Ca 197.8 mg, Zn 5.4 mg, Fe 10.3 mg, Folate 282.3 mcg, Na 229.6 mg, Suc 6.2 g

◇Stuffed Onion

Onions make a surprisingly good container for all kinds of stuffings flavored with the chopped center. In this case, I used spinach and mushrooms, dark vegetables to contrast with the pale onion.

1 jalapeño pepper
2 bay leaves
4 cloves
2 ¾-pound onions
¾ pound trimmed spinach leaves
2 teaspoons olive oil
½ pound mushrooms (regular, chanterelle, shiitake, etc.), roughly chopped into ½- to ⅓-inch pieces
2 tablespoons whole-wheat bread crumbs
2 tablespoons Chicken Stock or water

Cut enough flesh from the jalapeño pepper to make 1 minced table-spoon. Put the rest of it, including the seeds and core, in a pot with the bay leaves, cloves, peeled onions, and enough water to cover them. Bring to a boil and cook until the onions are almost soft, about 30 minutes. Drain and let cool. Discard the bay leaves and cloves.

Bring the water back to a boil. Add the spinach and cook for 1 minute. Drain, cool, and squeeze dry. Place in a bowl.

Preheat the oven to 350° F.

Cut each onion in half crosswise. Cut off the root ends. Pull out the center of each half until you have 4 onion cups about 4 layers thick. Cover the bottoms with some of the trimmings so they are as thick as the sides. Roughly chop the rest of the onion and set it aside.

Heat the oil in an 8-inch nonstick skillet. Add the chopped onion and cook for about 2 minutes, until lightly browned. Add the jalapeño pep-per and cook another minute. Add the mushrooms and cook until soft, another 2 to 3 minutes. Put in the bowl with the spinach and the bread crumbs.

Place the onion cups in a 9-inch pie plate or other baking dish large enough to hold them firmly in a single layer. Fill each cup with a fourth of the spinach mixture. Pour the stock or water into the bottom of the plate. Cover the plate with foil and bake in the preheated oven for 20 minutes. Once or twice during cooking, spoon the liquid in the pan over the onions.

Serves 4

◇Grilled Breast of Pigeon with Red Wine Sauce

Although we call it game, the pigeon we get today is domesticated. I usually cook just the breasts because there isn't much meat on the rest of these small birds.

4 1-pound pigeons
10 juniper berries
1 teaspoon coriander seed
½ teaspoon black peppercorns
2 cloves garlic, minced
Water or Vegetable Stock
1 pound sugar snap peas
¼ pound fresh whole-wheat fettuccine
½ cup dry red wine
2 cups Pigeon Stock (see below)
⅓ cup (1 ounce) diced celery
½ cup (1 ounce) diced leek
½ jalapeño pepper
3 ounces meat from cooked calf's foot, diced (meat is reserved from Pigeon Stock)
3 tablespoons diced tomato
¼ cup diced green bell pepper
2 teaspoons olive oil

Cut the breast pieces from each pigeon, scraping against the breast bone with your knife. Remove and discard the skin. Use the bones and innards, except the livers, to make the stock along with the other ingredients listed in the stock recipe that follows.

In a small spice or coffee grinder, grind together the juniper, coriander, and peppercorns. Rub them over the breasts along with half the minced garlic. Set aside to marinate while the stock cooks.

Bring a pot of water or vegetable stock to a boil. Add the sugar snap peas and cook until barely done, about 2 minutes. Drain well and set aside. Keep warm.

Bring the liquid back to a boil and add the fettuccine. Cook for about 3 minutes, or until barely done. Drain well. Keep warm.

Bring the red wine to a boil in a saucepan. Cook until reduced to a glaze. Add the pigeon stock and cook until reduced to ¾ cup. Add the celery, leek, jalapeño pepper, remaining garlic, and calf's foot meat. Cook over high heat for 4 to 5 minutes. Add the tomato and bell pepper. Cook 2 minutes longer, or until the sauce is thick.

Heat a grill until hot or heat the oil in a nonstick skillet. Add the pigeon breasts and cook over high heat for about 3 minutes per side. If grilling, sear the first side, then rotate it 45 degrees and return to the grill, same side down, to give each piece a diamond pattern. Turn and finish cooking on the other side.

Spoon some sauce onto the center of each of 4 dinner plates. Arrange 2 breast halves over each so they form a sort of **V**. Place some of the fettuccine between them and some sugar snap peas around the edge. Serve the remaining peas and pasta on the side.

If you prefer, place the pigeon breasts overlapping on a serving platter. Put the sugar snap peas on one side, the fettuccine on the other, and serve the sauce on the side in a sauceboat.

Serves 4

◇Pigeon Stock

Since pigeons are small, the bones and trimmings won't make much stock. I add a calf's foot, rich in gelatin, and use the meat in the sauce.

Bones and legs from 4 pigeons, skin removed
1 pound calf's foot, split
1 ¼-pound onion, quartered
¼ pound mushroom stems
6 ounces carrots, quartered
2 stalks celery, quartered
1 ¼-pound parsnip, quartered
3 cloves garlic
2 bay leaves
6 cloves
3 fresh sage leaves
1 sprig fresh rosemary
1 dried red chili pepper

Place everything in a stockpot. Cover with water and bring to a boil. Remove and discard any scum and fat that rise to the surface. Lower the heat so the liquid is at a steady simmer. Partially cover and cook for 3 hours. Check the pot from time to time, removing fat and scum as needed.

When the stock is done, pour it through a sieve lined with a dampened kitchen towel. Discard all the solids except the calf's foot. Pour the stock into a clean pot and reduce by boiling, uncovered, over moderate heat until you have 2 cups. Cube the meat from the calf's foot and use it in the recipe for the grilled pigeon breasts.

◇Green Gazpacho
◇Stuffed Breast of Pheasant

The gazpacho, almost a salad in a soup bowl, is a cooling start. Make it a day ahead at the same time you stuff the pheasant.

Green Gazpacho   CAL 149

Pro 4.6 g, Cho 15.5 g, Fat 7.5 g, Sat 0.9 g, Chol 0.2 mg, Fiber 2.1 g, Ca 99.7 mg, Zn 0.8 mg, Fe 3.4 mg, Folate 86 mcg, Na 127.6 mg, Suc 0.7 g

Stuffed Breast of Pheasant   CAL 462

Pro 36 g, Cho 29.2 g, Fat 16.5 g, Sat 2 g, Chol 111 mg, Fiber 1.3 g, Ca 43.2 mg, Zn 4.2 mg, Fe 4.8 mg, Folate 35.9 mcg, Na 167.5 mg, Suc 0.6 g

Total Menu   CAL 611

Pro 40.6 g, Cho 44.7 g, Fat 24 g, Sat 2.9 g, Chol 111.2 mg, Fiber 3.4 g, Ca 142.9 mg, Zn 5 mg, Fe 8.2 mg, Folate 121.9 mcg, Na 295.1 mg, Suc 1.3 g

◇Green Gazpacho

Gazpacho, the raw vegetable soup of Spain, is usually made with red tomatoes. As a variation, I make this with unripe green tomato and a range of green vegetables. The only red is in the cubes of bell pepper that garnish the soup, making a pleasing contrast.

Most gazpachos are chunky. This is a smooth version. The texture becomes much finer in a blender than in a food processor, although a food processor will work nearly as well.

1 bunch (1 ounce) parsley leaves
1 ounce arugula leaves
1 ounce watercress leaves
2 ounces spinach leaves
1 2-ounce onion
1 medium (5-ounce) green bell pepper
2 large (2-ounce) stalks celery
1 small (¼-pound) unripe green tomato, cored
1 large (½-pound) cucumber (preferably unwaxed so it doesn't have to be peeled)
1 jalapeño pepper, cored and seeded
1 tablespoon chopped fresh dill
1 pinch oregano, preferably fresh
1 cup Chicken Stock
Juice of 1 lemon
2 tablespoons olive oil
Freshly ground black pepper
½ red bell pepper, cored, seeded, and cut into ¼-inch squares
1 slice whole wheat bread, cut into ¼-inch cubes, toasted

Bring a large pot of water to a boil. Add the parsley, arugula, watercress, spinach, and onion. Cook for 1 minute. Drain and squeeze dry.

Roughly chop the green pepper, celery, onion, green tomato, cucumber, and jalapeño pepper. Place them in a blender or food processor with the blanched vegetables, dill, and oregano. If you are using a blender, you will have to work in 2 batches. Run the machine until everything is well pureed. Add the chicken stock, lemon juice, olive oil, and black pepper; continue pureeing until smooth. Press through a fine strainer.

Chill thoroughly before serving. Top each portion with some of the red bell pepper and whole-wheat croutons.

Serves 4

◇Stuffed Breast of Pheasant

The pheasant surrounds the strips of bright vegetables, allowing them to flavor each other as they steam. The plastic wrap keeps the juices in without affecting the flavor. If you can't get pheasant, chicken breasts are a fine substitute.

4 ¼-pound boneless, skinless pheasant breasts
8 ¼-inch-wide red bell pepper strips
8 ¼-inch-wide yellow bell pepper strips
8 ¼-inch-wide green bell pepper strips
8 ¼-inch-wide 4- to 5-inch carrot strips, blanched
8 string beans (2 ounces), blanched
1 teaspoon minced fresh ginger
1½ teaspoons minced jalapeño pepper
8 fresh sage leaves, or ½ teaspoon dried sage
2 cups Pheasant Stock (see below), reduced to 1 cup
1 tablespoon unsalted butter
1 tablespoon all-purpose flour
2 tablespoons chopped fresh chives
1 teaspoon fresh lemon juice
Freshly ground black pepper
1 recipe Wild Rice (see page 90), made with Pheasant Stock instead
    of Chicken Stock

Place each pheasant breast between 2 sheets of waxed paper and pound with a meat pounder or heavy pot until about ¼ inch thick. Place a fourth of the bell peppers, carrots, and string beans lengthwise in the center of each breast so the vegetables all go in the same direction. Sprinkle with the ginger, jalapeño pepper, and sage. Fold the pheasant edges over to cover the vegetables, then roll up so none of the vegetables show.

Place each roll on good-quality plastic wrap, fold over the bottom, fold in the sides, and roll up to make a very tight package. Cut the excess plastic. (This is easiest if you have someone to help who can keep the plastic taut as you work.) Place the roll in the center of a second sheet of plastic and roll it the opposite way to make a tight seal. You can make the packages ahead and refrigerate until cooking time.

Bring some water or the liquid you used to blanch the vegetables to a boil in the bottom of a steamer or wok. Place the pheasant rolls on a steamer rack over the boiling liquid. Cover and cook for about 15 minutes. Remove to a plate. Place something under part of the plate so it sits at an angle. With scissors, snip a small hole in each package so the excess liquid runs out. Catch the liquid and add it to the reduced pheasant stock.

Heat the stock in a saucepan. Put the butter and flour in a small bowl and mix them with a fork or your fingers to make a smooth paste. This is called beurre manié. Whisk it into the sauce, stirring vigorously until the sauce is smooth and thick. Cook just to heat through. Stir in the chives, lemon juice, and black pepper to taste. Keep warm.

Cut the plastic wrap away from each pheasant roll. Trim the very tips off to expose the vegetables. Then slice each roll on the diagonal into 4 or 5 pieces. Arrange them overlapping on individual plates. Spoon some of the sauce on top. Spoon the wild rice next to it.

Serves 4

◇Pheasant Stock

The best part of the pheasant is the breast. Cut the breast meat away and use it to make the Stuffed Breast of Pheasant or another pheasant recipe. Discard the skin along with any obvious fat and break up the carcass for the stock.

4 pounds pheasant bones and trims
6 ounces onion, quartered
6 ounces carrots
6 ounces leek greens
6 ounces parsnips
4 cloves garlic
3 ounces parsley stems
1 dried red chili pepper
2 bay leaves
6 cloves
12 toasted juniper berries (see note)
1 cup dry vermouth

Place the pheasant bones in a stockpot. Cover with water and bring to a boil. Pour out the water and rinse off the bones. Rinse out the pot and return the bones to it with all the remaining ingredients. Add enough cold water to just cover everything.

Bring the liquid back to a boil. Remove and discard any scum and fat that rise to the surface. Lower the heat so the liquid is at a steady simmer. Partially cover and cook for 3 hours. Check the pot from time to time, removing fat and scum as needed.

When the stock is done, pour it through a sieve lined with a dampened kitchen towel. Discard all the solids. The vegetables won't have much flavor because they will have given it to the stock. Pour the stock into a clean pot and reduce by boiling, uncovered, over moderate heat until you have 1 quart (4 cups).

NOTE: To toast the juniper berries, put them in a dry skillet and cook over moderate heat, shaking the pan, for a few minutes.

◇Sliced Mushrooms on Wild Rice
◇Stuffed Spring Cabbage with Rabbit

Growing up in Switzerland, I ate rabbit frequently and am pleased to see that it is slowly gaining popularity here. Most of what we get comes from Arkansas or Canada and is very tender and tasty, more interesting than chicken. This stuffed cabbage makes a satisfying main course after the mushrooms and rice.

Prepare the rabbit ahead and reheat. Make the mushrooms just before serving.

Sliced Mushrooms on Wild Rice   CAL 301

Pro 10.5 g, Cho 31.6 g, Fat 12.8 g, Sat 3.2 g, Chol 11.4 mg, Fiber 1.4 g, Ca 71.5 mg, Zn 1.7 mg, Fe 3.5 mg, Folate 46.2 mcg, Na 80.6 mg, Suc 0.4 g

Stuffed Spring Cabbage with Rabbit

CAL 320

Pro 31.1 g, Cho 12.8 g, Fat 10.1 g, Sat 3.8 g, Chol 87.3 mg, Fiber 1.4 g, Ca 84.2 mg, Zn 3 mg, Fe 3.7 mg, Folate 57.1 mcg, Na 128.8 mg, Suc 3.8 g

Total Menu   CAL 621

Pro 41.6 g, Cho 44.4 g, Fat 22.9 g, Sat 7 g, Chol 98.7 mg, Fiber 2.8 g, Ca 155.7 mg, Zn 4.7 mg, Fe 7.2 mg, Folate 103.3 mcg, Na 209.4 mg, Suc 4.2 g

◇Sliced Mushrooms on Wild Rice

The woodsy taste of the mushrooms is a perfect complement to that of the rice.

1 tablespoon corn oil
1 clove garlic, minced
½ cup sliced shallots
2 bay leaves
¾ pound assorted mushrooms (including shiitake and chanterelles if available), sliced
2 tablespoons water
¼ cup chopped fresh parsley
¼ cup chopped fresh chives
½ cup low-fat sour cream
1 recipe Wild Rice (see page 90)

Heat the oil in a wok. Add the garlic, shallots, and bay leaves. Cook until lightly browned, about 2 minutes. Remove and discard the bay leaves. Add the mushrooms and water. Cover and cook until the mushrooms are soft, about 5 minutes. Add the parsley and chives. Cover again and cook 1 minute longer. Remove from the heat and stir in the sour cream, letting bits of it show.

Spoon some wild rice in a circle on each plate. Top with some of the mushroom mixture.

Serves 4

◇Stuffed Spring Cabbage with Rabbit

Cabbage is an excellent casing for all kinds of mixtures—from lobster and beef to this rabbit stew. The golden saffron filling peeks through the transparent green leaves.

1 2½-pound rabbit
¼ pound carrots, cut into large chunks
½ large onion, halved
1 stalk celery, halved
1 large leek, root off, washed, halved
¼ pound turnips, halved
1 clove garlic
½ jalapeño pepper, cored and seeded
1 small bay leaf
2 cloves
1 pinch saffron
1 cup dry white wine
8 large spring or savoy cabbage leaves
1 cup Rabbit Stock (see below)
Freshly ground black pepper

Skin and bone the rabbit, reserving the bones for the stock. Discard the heart. Save the liver for the sauce. Cut the meat into 1-inch cubes, trimming off any fat. You should have about 18 ounces of meat.

Put the rabbit in a 10-inch skillet with all but the last 3 ingredients. Add enough water to almost cover. Place over high heat and bring to a boil. Partially cover the pan. Lower the heat to a simmer. Let cook for about an hour. The rabbit should be tender.

Remove from the heat and let cool. Put everything into a sieve, reserving the liquid. Pick out the rabbit pieces and set them aside in a bowl. Pick out and discard the bay leaf and cloves. Put all the other solids and the liquid back in the skillet. Cook over high heat until the vegetables have absorbed all the liquid. Watch carefully toward the end to be sure they don't burn. When the liquid is gone, remove the mixture from the heat and let cool. Place all the vegetables in a food processor and process until smooth. Mix the pureed vegetables with the rabbit for the stuffing mixture.

Bring a large pot of water to a boil. Pare down the thick ribs of the cabbage leaves so they are fairly flat. Drop them into the boiling water and cook until soft, about 3 minutes. Depending on the cabbage, it may be difficult to remove whole leaves without tearing them. In that case, cut away the core and drop the whole cabbage into the boiling water. As outer leaves soften, pull them away. Continue until you have 8 large soft leaves. Save any smaller pieces to use to patch tears if necessary. Pare the ribs of the softened leaves.

Arrange 8 cabbage leaves, rib sides down, on your work surface. They should be about 6 inches wide and 7 inches long. If they are too big, trim them. If they are torn, patch them. Divide the filling among the leaves, putting it in a pile about a third of the way up each leaf. Fold the bottom over and then fold in the sides and roll up. Place the rolls, open side down, in a 12-inch gratin dish. Mix up the various shades of green to make an attractive pattern. Pour ¼ cup stock in the dish and cover with foil. This can be done the day ahead and refrigerated.

When ready to serve, bring the gratin dish to room temperature. Preheat the oven to 350° F. Put the stuffed cabbage in the oven to heat through, about 15 minutes.

While the cabbage is heating, bring the remaining ¾ cup stock to a boil. Add the reserved rabbit liver, lower the heat, and simmer until cooked through, about 7 minutes. Put the liver and stock in a food processor and process until smooth. Press through a fine sieve to make a silky sauce. Season to taste with freshly ground black pepper and serve with the cabbage rolls.

Serves 4

◇Rabbit Stock

Bones and trims from 2½-pound rabbit
2 ounces onion
2 ounces leek greens
2 ounces carrot
2 ounces celery root
1 ounce parsley stems
½ jalapeño pepper
1 teaspoon coriander seed
Sprig fresh thyme
2 fresh sage leaves

Place the bones in a stockpot. Cover with water and bring to a boil. Pour out the water. Rinse the scum off the bones and pot. Return the bones to the pot with all the remaining ingredients. Add enough cold water to just cover everything.

Bring the liquid back to a boil. Remove and discard any scum and fat that rise to the surface. Lower the heat so the liquid is at a steady simmer. Partially cover and cook for 2 hours. Check the pot from time to time, removing fat and scum as needed.

When the stock is done, pour it through a sieve lined with a dampened kitchen towel. Discard all the solids. Pour the stock into a clean pot and reduce by boiling, uncovered, over moderate heat until you have 1 cup.

◇Marinated Bay Scallops with Cilantro
◇Medallion of Buffalo with Wild Mushrooms

The cool, lemony flavor of the scallops bathed in pepper puree complements the hearty buffalo with mushrooms and wild rice. Marinate the scallops and make their sauce ahead.

Marinated Bay Scallops with Cilantro

CAL 81

Pro 7.4 g, Cho 10.5 g, Fat 2.4 g, Sat 0.2 g, Chol 13.4 mg, Fiber 1.2 g, Ca 64 mg, Zn 0.5 mg, Fe 2 mg, Folate 26.6 mcg, Na 79.7 mg, Suc 0.3 g

Medallion of Buffalo with Wild Mushrooms

CAL 570

Pro 37.3 g, Cho 40.1 g, Fat 20.6 g, Sat 5.2 g, Chol 72.9 mg, Fiber 2 g, Ca 83.1 mg, Zn 5.2 mg, Fe 8.5 g, Folate 58.6 mcg, Na 175.6 mg, Suc 1.8 g

Total Menu   CAL 651

Pro 44.7 g, Cho 50.6 g, Fat 23 g, Sat 5.4 g, Chol 86.3 mg, Fiber 3.2 g, Ca 147.1 mg, Zn 5.7 mg, Fe 10.5 mg, Folate 85.2 mcg, Na 255.3 mg, Suc 2.1 g

◇Marinated Bay Scallops with Cilantro

This very simple dish is similar to seviche but the scallops are given a silky yellow sauce.

6 ounces bay scallops
½ cup fresh lemon juice
2 jalapeño peppers, halved
3 tablespoons lime juice
½ recipe Yellow Pepper Puree Sauce (see page 28)
Freshly ground black pepper
¼ cup chopped cilantro (fresh coriander)

Pull off and discard the tough muscles on each scallop, then place the scallops in a bowl with the lemon juice and jalapeño peppers. Refrigerate overnight. The acid in the lemon juice will "cook" the scallops.

When you are ready to serve, drain the scallops. Divide them among 4 coquille shells or other small serving dishes. Add the lime juice to the yellow pepper puree and spoon it over the scallops. Grind black pepper on top and sprinkle with the cilantro.

Serves 4

◇Medallion of Buffalo with Wild Mushrooms

Buffalo is growing in popularity with the interest in American foods. It also has the advantage of being lower in cholesterol than beef. Of course, if you can't find buffalo, beef tenderloin will be fine. Either way, this is the kind of filling dish sure to please the heartiest eaters you know.

1 pound buffalo tenderloin, all fat removed
Freshly ground black pepper
2 teaspoons dried thyme
2 tablespoons corn oil
2 tablespoons minced shallots
¼ cup dry red wine
2 tablespoons bourbon
2 cups Beef or Veal Stock
½ cup minced onion
1 jalapeño pepper, cored, seeded, and minced
¼ cup chopped fresh chives or scallion greens
¼ cup chopped fresh parsley
1 pound mushrooms (fresh shiitake, chanterelle, button, etc.), sliced or quartered
¼ cup low-fat sour cream
1 recipe Wild Rice (see page 90)

Cut the buffalo into 8 rounds, each weighing 2 ounces. Rub freshly ground black pepper, thyme, and 1 teaspoon oil over the meat.

In a 10-inch nonstick or well-seasoned iron skillet, heat 2 teaspoons oil. When the pan is hot, add the meat. It should fit in one layer so it can all brown. When well browned on the bottom, turn the meat over and cook the other side. Total cooking time should be about 3 minutes for rare. Remove the meat to a heated platter and keep warm.

Add the shallots to the pan, followed by the wine, bourbon, and stock. Scrape the pan with a wooden spoon to deglaze. Bring the liquid to a boil and cook for a few minutes to thicken. Pour the sauce over the meat. Return it to its warm place.

Heat the remaining tablespoon oil in the same skillet. Add the onion, jalapeño pepper, chives, and parsley. Cook until lightly browned. Add the mushrooms and cook until soft, about 2 minutes. If they don't give off any liquid at first, sprinkle a few drops of water into the pan to create steam. Stir in the sour cream. When blended and heated through, remove from the heat.

Serve the mushrooms and wild rice with the medallions of buffalo.

Serves 4

◇Seviche of Striped Bass with Orange
◇Grilled Venison Chops with Stewed Chestnuts and Dried Fruit

The white fish specked with green served in an orange shell is a light start, followed by robust venison chops with stewed fruits. Marinate the seviche and cook the fruits and chestnuts ahead to reheat when you cook the venison. Assemble the oranges just before serving.

Seviche of Striped Bass with Orange

CAL 221

Pro 20.2 g, Cho 31.5 g, Fat 3.1 g, Sat 1 g, Chol 46.9 mg, Fiber 1.5 g, Ca 129.1 mg, Zn 1.3 mg, Fe 2.6 mg, Folate 130.5 mcg, Na 66.2 mg, Suc 9.1 g

Grilled Venison Chops with Stewed Chestnuts and Dried Fruit   CAL 400

Pro 27.8 g, Cho 49.7 g, Fat 7.4 g, Sat 3.1 g, Chol 73.9 mg, Fiber 2.3 g, Ca 60.9 mg, Zn 4 mg, Fe 5.4 mg, Folate 10.4 mcg, Na 155.4 mg, Suc 8.4 g

Total Menu   CAL 621

Pro 48 g, Cho 81.2 g, Fat 10.5 g, Sat 4.1 g, Chol 120.8 mg, Fiber 3.8 g, Ca 190 mg, Zn 5.3 mg, Fe 8 mg, Folate 140.9 mcg, Na 221.6 mg, Suc 17.5 g

◇Seviche of Striped Bass with Orange

The firm white fish contrasts well with the orange sections and cups, set off by the green cilantro and 2-Mamina. If you have access to bitter or blood oranges, use them for this dish in place of the navel oranges.

3/4 pound skinless striped bass fillets
1/4 cup fresh lemon juice
2 tablespoons fresh lime juice
6 navel oranges
1/4 cup red bell pepper, cored, seeded, and cut into narrow 1-inch-long strips
1/4 cup green bell pepper, cored, seeded, and cut into narrow 1-inch-long strips
1/3 cup thinly sliced red onion
1 1/2 teaspoons minced jalapeño pepper
2 tablespoons minced cilantro (fresh coriander)
1/2 teaspoon ground cumin
1 2.5-ounce package 2-Mamina (Japanese radish sprouts)

Cut the bass fillets in half along the center membrane. Slice each piece crosswise into strips about ¼ inch wide. Place them in a bowl with the lemon and lime juices. Stir so the juice coats all the fish. Cover and refrigerate overnight. If you want to serve the fish the same day, leave it at room temperature for 6 hours. When the fish has marinated enough, it will be opaque and firm like cooked fish.

Cut 4 oranges in two so that the bottom is slightly larger than the top. Squeeze the juice from the tops into a measuring cup. With a small knife or pointed spoon, carefully remove the pulp from the bottoms without breaking the rind. Squeeze as much of the pulp as you need to make a cup of juice.

Cut a thin slice off the bottom of the 4 orange shells so they will sit flat on plates. Set the shells aside.

With a knife, cut the rind and all the pith from the remaining 2 oranges, then cut them into their natural sections, leaving the membranes behind.

Strain the orange juice, discarding the pulp. Mix it with the red and green peppers, red onion, jalapeño pepper, cilantro, and cumin. Stir in half the orange sections.

Shortly before serving, put the marinated fish into a strainer to eliminate excess liquid. Combine the fish with the orange juice mixture. Spoon equal amounts of the sauced fish into the orange shells and place them on individual plates. Garnish with some 2-Mamina. Arrange the remaining orange sections and 2-Mamina around each orange shell.

Serves 4

◇Grilled Venison Chops with Stewed Chestnuts and Dried Fruit

The dried fruits and chestnuts make a wonderful winter side dish with turkey or goose as well as the venison. It is a good idea to roast a few extra chestnuts. Some may be moldy and you won't know until you peel them.

12 chestnuts (4 ounces)

1 large (8-ounce) apple, peeled, cored, and quartered

2 ounces dried figs

2 ounces dried apricots

3 ounces prunes

1 dried red chili pepper

½ cup Chicken Stock

2 teaspoons freshly ground black pepper

2 teaspoons ground toasted juniper berries (see note)

1½ teaspoons olive oil

8 venison chops, cut from the rack, trimmed of all fat (1 pound meat)

2 cups Beef Stock reduced to ¾ cup

1 teaspoon arrowroot dissolved in 1 teaspoon water

Preheat the oven to 450° F.

With a sharp paring or razor-tipped knife, cut around each chestnut through the shell in a ring about a third of the way down from the root end. Spread the chestnuts in a pan and bake in the preheated oven for about 10 minutes. The chestnuts should be cooked and the shell loose enough to peel away easily.

Place the peeled chestnuts in a 2-quart pot with the apple, figs, apricots, prunes, chili pepper, and chicken stock. Bring the liquid to a boil. Cover, lower the heat, and cook for about 30 minutes. All the liquid should be absorbed and the fruit soft but still in large pieces. Keep warm.

Heat a grill or broiler.

Combine the ground pepper and juniper in a small bowl. Put the olive oil on a plate. Turn each chop in the oiled plate, then sprinkle ⅛ teaspoon pepper mixture on each side. Place them on the hot grill or under the broiler. Cook 1 minute per side for rare.

Bring the reduced stock to a boil and stir in the dissolved arrowroot. Cook a moment until the sauce thickens. Season it with freshly ground black pepper.

Serve 2 chops per person with some of the sauce and the dried fruits on the side.

Serves 4

NOTE: To toast juniper berries, put them in a dry skillet and cook over moderate heat, shaking the pan, for a few minutes.

Stocks

Good stocks are essentials in my kitchen, especially when I make Spa Cuisine dishes that require intense flavors to make up for the lack of salt. Making stock takes some time but it is not difficult, nor need it be very exact. Make it on a day when you are going to be in the kitchen anyway. All you really need are bones and water although vegetables add to the full taste. I always add garlic. Years ago, my father told me that for every clove of garlic in the stock, you can use one less pound of meat. To make really good stocks, I use both.

In the restaurant, of course, I have a ready supply of vegetables. I also add vegetable trimmings to the pot. When you plan to make stock, save your trimmings. It is also a good way to get rid of old carrots, limp celery, the odd onion, parsley stems, leek and scallion greens. It is better not to peel the vegetables since there is flavor and nutrition in the skins (besides, it's easier). Since they will cook for hours, leave them in large pieces or they will disintegrate before the stock is done.

Always use cold water to make stock. It pulls the flavor from the bones and vegetables as they cook. Hot water seals the flavors in. That is why you want simmering water to poach a chicken or fish.

The absence of salt in the stock recipes is not just because they are for Spa Cuisine. I never add salt to any stock until I am ready to use it. Bones have natural sodium that intensifies as the stock reduces. If I added salt at the beginning, the end result would often be too salty.

The recipes in this section are for basic stocks each used in more than one recipe. Those used only once are included in the appropriate menu.

There are canned stocks on the market that can do if necessary. Remember, however, that most have salt in them. I urge you to make your own stocks. Double or triple the recipe and freeze what you make in 1- or 2-cup containers, ready for a single recipe. They will last for months in the freezer. Each stock recipe makes a quart.

◇Beef Stock

Because beef stock is best dark, I brown the bones and onion under the broiler before adding them to the stock pot.

1 6-ounce onion
4 pounds beef bones
6 ounces leek, in 2-inch pieces
6 ounces celery or celery root, halved
6 ounces parsnips, halved
4 cloves garlic
2 bay leaves
6 cloves
1 tablespoon white peppercorns
2 cups dry white wine
½ teaspoon dried sage

Heat the broiler. Cut the onion, skin still on, in half. Place it under the broiler with the beef bones until lightly burnt. Set aside.

Place the bones in a stockpot. Cover with water and bring to a boil. Pour out the water. Rinse off the bones. Rinse out the pot and return the bones to it with all the remaining ingredients, including the burnt onion. Add enough cold water to just cover everything.

Bring the liquid back to a boil. Remove and discard any scum and fat that rise to the surface. Lower the heat so the liquid is at a steady simmer. Partially cover and cook for 6 hours. Check the pot from time to time, removing fat and scum as needed.

When the stock is done, pour it through a sieve lined with a dampened kitchen towel. Discard all the solids. The vegetables won't have much flavor because they will have given it to the stock. Pour the stock into a clean pot and reduce by boiling, uncovered, over moderate heat until you have 1 quart (4 cups).

◇Chicken Stock

If you make chicken often, save all the trims—bones from the breasts, wing tips, backbones, necks, etc. Put them in the freezer and make stock when you have enough.

4 pounds chicken backs and necks
6 ounces onion, halved
6 ounces celery, halved
6 cloves garlic
6 ounces leek greens, in 2-inch pieces
6 ounces carrots, halved
1 teaspoon rosemary, preferably fresh
2 bay leaves
4 cloves

Place the chicken in a stockpot. Cover with water and bring to a boil. Pour out the water. Rinse off the bones. Rinse out the pot and return the chicken to it with all the remaining ingredients. Add enough cold water to just cover everything.

Bring the liquid back to a boil. Remove and discard any scum and fat that rise to the surface. Lower the heat so the liquid is at a steady simmer. Partially cover and cook for 3 hours. Check the pot from time to time, removing fat and scum as needed.

When the stock is done, pour it through a sieve lined with a dampened kitchen towel. Discard all the solids. The vegetables won't have much flavor because they will have given it to the stock. Pour the stock into a clean pot and reduce by boiling, uncovered, over moderate heat until you have 1 quart (4 cups).

◇Fish Stock

Fish bones, being smaller, cook much faster than other bones. Consequently, cut the vegetables smaller or they will not be done when the stock is. Be sure to wash all the blood off the bones and heads or it will discolor the stock and make it bitter.

4 pounds bones and heads from lean fish (striped bass, snapper.
    trout, cod, etc., but no oily fish)
10 ounces onion
½ pound leek whites
¼ pound celery root or celery
6 ounces parsnips
6 ounces fennel bulb
2 sticks dried fennel
6 cloves garlic
4 sprigs fresh chervil, or 1 teaspoon dried chervil
3 bay leaves
1 teaspoon coriander seed
1 teaspoon dried marjoram
1 cup dry vermouth
1 dried red chili pepper

Wash the fish bones and heads to remove all traces of blood. Place the bones and heads in a stockpot. Cover with water and bring to a boil. Pour out the water. Rinse off the bones. Rinse out the pot and return the bones to it with all the remaining ingredients. Add enough cold water to just cover everything.

Bring the liquid back to a boil. Remove and discard any scum and fat that rise to the surface. Lower the heat so the liquid is at a steady simmer. Partially cover and cook for 1 hour. Check the pot from time to time, removing fat and scum as needed.

When the stock is done, pour it through a sieve lined with a dampened kitchen towel. Discard all the solids. The vegetables won't have much flavor because they will have given it to the stock. Pour the stock into a clean pot and reduce by boiling, uncovered, over moderate heat until you have 1 quart (4 cups).

◇Lamb Stock

Lamb stock is not an all-purpose stock, like beef or chicken. If you make any of the dishes using loin of lamb, you will probably have to buy a whole saddle. Cut the loin and fillets from the bones to use in the recipes. Trim the fat from the flaps and discard, saving the meat for the stock along with the bones. If you get your butcher to do the boning for you, ask him to cut up the bones with his saw into 4-inch pieces.

6 ounces onion

4 pounds lamb bones and trimmings

6 ounces leek greens, in 2-inch pieces

6 ounces celery, halved

6 ounces parsnips, halved

6 ounces white turnips, halved

1 ounce cilantro (fresh coriander) stems

8 cloves garlic

1 teaspoon coriander seed

4 sprigs fresh tarragon, or ½ teaspoon dried tarragon

1 tablespoon black peppercorns

2 bay leaves

6 cloves

2 cups red wine

Heat the broiler. Cut the onion, skin still on, in half. Place it under the broiler with the lamb bones until lightly burnt. Set aside.

Place the bones in a stockpot. Cover with water and bring to a boil. Pour out the water. Rinse off the bones. Rinse out the pot and return the bones to it with all the remaining ingredients. Add enough cold water to just cover everything.

Bring the liquid back to a boil. Remove and discard any scum and fat that rise to the surface. Lower the heat so the liquid is at a steady simmer. Partially cover and cook for 4 hours. Check the pot from time to time, removing fat and scum as needed.

When the stock is done, pour it through a sieve lined with a dampened kitchen towel. Discard all the solids. The vegetables won't have much flavor because they will have given it to the stock. Pour the stock into a clean pot and reduce by boiling, uncovered, over moderate heat until you have 1 quart (4 cups).

◇Veal Stock

If you only make one stock, this is probably the most versatile, fine for beef, veal, lamb, and chicken dishes.

4 pounds veal bones (preferably from the shank)
6 ounces onion, quartered
6 ounces leek greens, in 2-inch pieces
6 ounces celery, halved
6 ounces carrots, cut in thirds
6 ounces parsnips, halved
2 ounces parsley stems
4 cloves garlic
2 bay leaves
6 cloves
1 tablespoon white peppercorns
2 cups dry white wine
1 fresh sage leaf or ½ teaspoon dried sage

Place the bones in a stockpot. Cover with water and bring to a boil. Pour out the water. Rinse off the bones. Rinse out the pot and return the bones to it with all the remaining ingredients, including the burnt onion. Add enough cold water to just cover everything.

Bring the liquid back to a boil. Remove and discard any scum and fat that rise to the surface. Lower the heat so the liquid is a steady simmer. Partially cover and cook for 4 hours. Check the pot from time to time, removing fat and scum as needed.

When the stock is done, pour it through a sieve lined with a dampened kitchen towel. Discard all the solids. The vegetables won't have much flavor because they will have given it to the stock. Pour the stock into a clean pot and reduce by boiling, uncovered, over moderate heat until you have 1 quart (4 cups).

◇Vegetable Stock

In general, I prefer the full flavor of meat and fish stock to that made with just vegetables. When cooking for Spa Cuisine, in particular, I always seek maximum flavor from all ingredients, especially liquids. I get some of it from impromptu vegetable stocks. Before steaming or blanching vegetables or completed dishes, I add scraps to the water. They might be carrot peelings, ends of zucchini, the ribs of bell peppers, bits of shallot or garlic, parsley stems. I might throw in a bay leaf or sprig of whatever herb is handy. If I've blanched vegetables earlier, I use the same liquid to cook pasta or steam chicken.

These stocks are not as intense as the long-cooking ones made with bones, so I don't save them for more than a day.

Index

Albin, Christian ("Hitch"), 15
anchovies, in Lindstrom steak, 220–21
apple(s) baked with red cabbage, 218–19
artichoke(s)
    and pepper salad, baked, 38–39
    stuffed: with mushrooms and bulgur, 60–
        61; with pork, 254–55
asparagus with red pepper sauce, 234–35
asparagus, wild: sautéed with crab, 166–
    167
aspic, seafood, 272–73
avocado
    determining ripeness of, 288
    in guacamole, 288–89
    with trout, 286–87

baked apples with red cabbage, 218–19
baked beefsteak tomato with goat cheese
    and corn, 100–101
baked pepper and artichoke salad, 38–39
baked swordfish steak with olives and
    scallions, 74–75
bami goreng, 72
barbecue, 238, 242–43
barley-mushroom soup, 248–49
basil with whole-wheat fettuccine and
    garlic, 66–67
bass, striped, see striped bass
bay scallops
    marinated, with cilantro, 318–19
    timbale of, in spinach, 26–27
bean(s), black: with squid salad, 160–61
bean(s), broad
    braised, 178–79
    in minestrone, 188–89
bean(s), green
    with spring lamb (fillet), 262–63
    with whole-wheat fettuccine, garlic,
        and basil, 66–67
beef
    boiled, 230–31
    carpaccio with striped bass and tuna
        sashimi, 140–41
    flank steak, stuffed (matembré), 196–
        197

grilled tenderloin, with lamb, veal, and
    braised lentils, 242–43
steak, see steak
stew, 236–37
stock, 330–31
beef, ground: as Lindstrom steak, 220–21
beef brisket
    in borscht, 120–21
    with stampot, 214–15
beer: beefsteak braised in, 226–27
beet(s)
    with apples and red cabbage, 218–19
    in borscht, 120–21
    salad: grated, raw, 260–61; with
        romaine, endive, and grapefruit, 194–
        195
beet(s), pickled: in Lindstrom steak, 220–
    221
black beans, see bean(s), black
bluepoint oysters with trout and herb
    sauce, 82–83
boiled beef, 230–31
bok choy with buckwheat noodles, 72–73
borscht, 120–21
braised beefsteak with beer and onion,
    226–27
braised broad beans, 178–79
braised fillet of red snapper
    with endive and leek, 40–41
    with spring onions, 48–49
braised lentils, 244–45
braised Swiss chard, 76–77
brisket of beef, with stampot, 214–15
broad beans, see bean(s), broad
broccoli and chicken, stir-fried, 128–29
brown rice, 276–77
brussels sprouts, in stampot, 214–15
buckwheat kernels, see kasha
buckwheat noodles (soba)
    with boiled beef, 230–31
    with chicken breasts, tomato, vinegar,
        96–97
    green tea flavor (cha soba): in chicken
        salad, 117; with wild mushrooms,
        266–67

About the Author

Born in Lucerne, Switzerland, Seppi Renggli apprenticed in Switzerland and gained his early professional experience also in Stockholm and Amsterdam. He was chef at the Hermitage in the Channel Islands and at various Caribbean hotels. Mr. Renggli has been with Restaurant Associates since 1966 and has been chef at The Four Seasons since 1973. His recipes are featured in *The Four Seasons Cookbook* (Simon & Schuster, 1981). He began to create the Spa Cuisine recipes for The Four Seasons' menu in 1984. Chef Renggli and his wife, Janey, have three children and reside in Rockland County, New York.